Slippery Men

Slippery Men

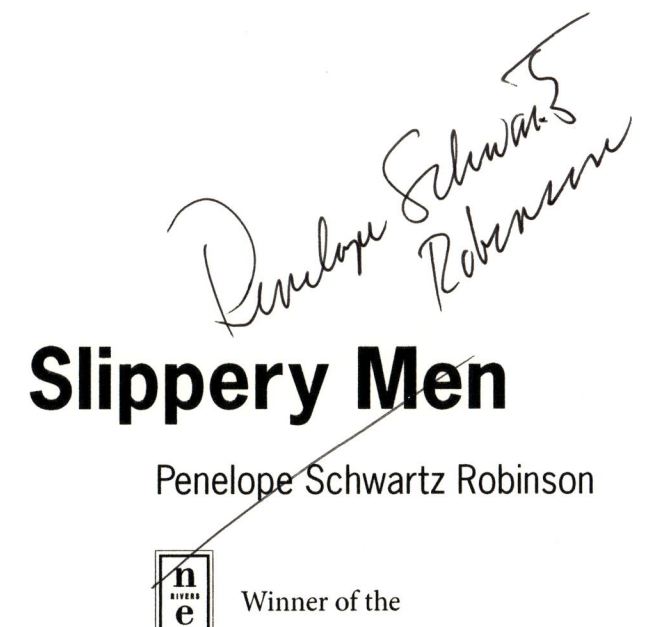

Penelope Schwartz Robinson

new

Winner of the
Stonecoast Book Prize

© 2008 by Penelope Schwartz Robinson
First Edition
Library of Congress Control Number: 2007936357
ISBN: 978-0-89823-242-4
The Stonecoast Book Prize
Cover design and interior book by Stephanie Thomas
Author photograph by Claudia Dricot

The publication of *Slippery Men* is made possible by the generous support of the McKnight Foundation, The Stonecoast M.F.A. Program at the University of Southern Maine, and other contributors to New Rivers Press.

For academic permission please contact Frederick T. Courtright at 570-839-7477 or permdude@eclipse.net. For all other permissions, contact The Copyright Clearance Center at 978-750-8400 or info@copyright.com.

New Rivers Press is a nonprofit literary press associated with Minnesota State University Moorhead.

Wayne Gudmundson, Director
Alan Davis, Senior Editor
Donna Carlson, Managing Editor
Thom Tammaro, Poetry Editor
Kevin Carollo, MVP Poetry Coordinator
Liz Severn, MVP Prose Coordinator
    Publishing Intern: Jennifer Bakken
    Honors Apprentice: Amanda Reiser
    Slippery Men Book Team: Amanda Huggett, Kellie Meehlhause, Ellie Musselman
    Editorial Interns: Janet Aarness, Ann Rosenquist Fee, Susan Flipp, Chris Hingley,
        Amanda Huggett, Steve Lauder, Brittany Mathiason, Kellie Meehlhause,
        Ellie Musselman, Rachel Roe, Kristen Underdahl
    Design Interns: Danielle DeKruif, Alison Eickhoff, Angelina Lennington,
        Kristen Stalboerger, Stephanie Thomas
    Festival Coordinator: Heather Steinmann
Allen Sheets, Design Manager
Deb Hval, Business Manager

Printed in the United States of America.

New Rivers Press
c/o MSUM
1104 7th Avenue South
Moorhead, MN 56563
www.newriverspress.com

For my family, near and far

Acknowledgments

The poet Sharon Olds wrote, "I was a late bloomer. But anyone who blooms at all, ever, is very lucky...." Amen. I didn't become serious about my writing until I was past the age of fifty, so I have a whole lifetime of experiences, luck, family, and friends who nurtured and nourished me along the way. I would not be writing this passage without every one of them.

   I certainly wouldn't be writing this passage without the Stonecoast Book Prize, which was the idea of Stonecoast faculty member and New Rivers Press Senior Editor Alan Davis. I am indebted to him as well as to Katha Pollitt, who selected my manuscript, and to the editing team at New Rivers Press who helped shepherd this collection into print. I am especially indebted to the Stonecoast MFA Program at the University of Southern Maine, which provided me the opportunity, creative community, and most importantly, dedicated faculty to develop my craft. I thank Barbara Hurd for her gentle yet fierce mentorship my first and last semesters, opening me up and bringing me home. I thank Richard Hoffman for his passion and commitment to my work, pushing me to places only he knew I could go. I am grateful to Laurie Stone for inspiring the title of this collection when she asked to see "more of those slippery men essays." And I thank my writing "sisters," Kim Dana Kupperman and Sarah Stromeyer, who have continued to anchor me to their hearts, guaranteeing a safe harbor. Marcia F. Brown, Corrie Calderwood, Leone Donovon, Sue William Silverman, Dustin Beall Smith, Jim Sprouse, Michael Steinberg, and Richard Wile all provided ongoing encouragement during and after Stonecoast.

My family has put up with a lot. I am enriched and inspired by my amazing daughters, Margaret Schwartz and Hilary Schwartz. I have been lucky to have known men who exposed me to ways of seeing and being I would otherwise never have experienced: my late husband, Harold Schwartz, for taking me to sea; Peter McHugh for showing me the back roads and upland country. My husband, Ed Robinson, is my constant and loving partner, forever my front man.

Finally, I want to thank Geri Mortenson, who listened to all of my words and took them to heart.

Slippery Men is a work of nonfiction. While the incidents described did occur, some of the names and personal characteristics of the individuals involved have been changed to protect their identities. Any resulting resemblance to persons living or dead is incidental or unintentional.

Contents

Lofting	15
Swiftwater	35
All Hands	43
Nat Leach Brook	63
When Lilacs Last	73
Hunting By Permission	109
Mucking About	129

Certain stages of experience might be compared with the game of Russian billiards, played ... on those small green tables, within the secret recesses of which, at the termination of a given passage of time ... the hidden gate goes down; after the descent of which, the coloured balls return no longer to be replayed; and all scoring is doubled. This is perhaps an image of how we live. For reasons not always at the time explicable, there are specific occasions when events begin suddenly to take on a significance previously unsuspected; so that, before we really know where we are, life seems to have begun in earnest at last, and we ourselves, scarcely aware that any change has taken place, are careering uncontrollably down the slippery avenues of eternity.

— Anthony Powell, *A Dance to the Music of Time,*
Volume II, *A Buyer's Market*

Lofting

I know a lot of secrets. People tell me things. They have to. It's part of my job. For years I've worked as a paralegal. When clients are getting divorced, I run their names through the EDGAR program. I find out which company boards they sit on or where they have stock options. I'm the instrument of full disclosure. I wend my way through the interstices of their financial lives, analyze their tax records, and trace the family trusts. Sometimes I need to sit down with the husband and explain that it will be possible to keep the ski condo if he gives up the deduction for the children. More often, I try to convince the wife that insisting upon having a particular rocking chair is not as important as taking a lump sum up front. Then they tell me things about each other: how he took unauthorized funds from the company, or how she slept with her sister's husband—the things I didn't need to know.

It's a small town. I think a lot about what I know about people that they don't know I know, about how it informs the way I deal with them; or don't. I wonder if they realize my secret is knowing their secrets. Or if it matters. Sometimes I pass a person on the street and imagine an aura around him of all the inner turmoil the world doesn't see. We smile and nod and I wonder if he believes his secrets are safe with me; or if he even thinks about his secrets when he sees me, as I think about his secrets when I see him. Maybe it doesn't occur to him that his secrets are spinning in my head, careering off another set of secrets from another aura encircling a person passing on my other side. Nine times out of ten, these secrets intertwine, creating a crosshatch of facts known and unknown, as unseen as neurofibrillary tangles in a brain scan signifying Alzheimer's. I walk through webs.

It happens all the time. I once worked on a case where a male college professor was accused of sexual harassment by a female employee of the school. She claimed he had raped her in his office; he claimed they had a long-standing consensual relationship, and she was angry when he ended it. To substantiate his story, he provided to our firm more than three hundred pages of e-mail between the two of them. There was no question but that they had shared an intimate, documented relationship. On the very evening of the afternoon she claimed he had forced her to perform fellatio under his desk, she sent him an e-mail saying "thank you for everything—even the dust balls in my hair." She blew it. I turned those e-mails into an exhibit for trial. I created a chronological spreadsheet identifying each sender, the subject of the message, its erotic content.

A recurrent theme in their e-mails was the Elmore James piece "If you don't like my peaches, please don't shake my tree." At a certain point, they probably would have called it "our song." One morning I stood behind the professor waiting in line at Starbucks. I knew him. He did not know me. The sensitive nature of the charge against him and his position in the community necessitated his meeting alone with his attorney at odd, often late, hours, his comings and goings identified as being social rather than business. He had no idea that within the dotted lines of the law firm—maybe on the other side of that very wall—I sifted though his e-mails, fashioning a chart of his love notes. Ahead of us in line, a young woman flirted with the man behind her. When he responded, she turned away as though she were insulted. The professor and I shared a knowing smile, and then I sing-songed, "If you don't like my peaches, please don't shake my tree." He laughed out loud—more like a bleat—and blushed. Only I knew why. And how complicated that flush of blood and emotion really was.

Or was I the only one? Who could tell? And why did I do that? I didn't intend to hurt him. But I couldn't resist heightening the situation just a little. That's what secrets do to you. They take on a life of their own. They cause you to poke at someone you would otherwise have given a friendly pat. Now one of the professor's secrets had morphed into a secret of mine. What could he have thought? Did he go away convinced there really is some mysterious symmetry in the world, whatever goes around comes around? Did he feel I had power over him? Did it make him believe in the cosmos?

I've been on the other side myself, when my telling secrets gave someone the power over me—as well as a whole town. And it didn't make me believe in the cosmos. It made me appreciate *hubris*. These secrets involve my naiveté, a man's guile, and the outcome of our social intercourse, which combined with arrogance to divide a righteous community. Am I making excuses already?

I was living in a rural place then, where my children attended nursery school upstairs in a village church. I was not a churchgoer, but this one came to have a good feel to me. To reach the Sunday school *cum* nursery school rooms on weekday mornings when I delivered my children, I had to walk through the vestry and down the red carpet toward the simple pine altar before a sky-blue nave. I began to feel expansive in that space. Uplifted. Soon I walked down the red carpet on Sundays too, when the church was full of people.

Maybe I was lonely. Perhaps, like many new mothers, I spent too much time with preschool children. In the country, community takes different forms, many of them assumed. I enjoyed the serenity, the singing, the fellowship of the Congregational Church.

The pastor appeared to be chiefly interested in the serenity, the singing, and the fellowship himself. The Reverend Homer Teach read a little Wordsworth, remarked how the sun set over the bay, and then lauded the choir. Because it was essentially nonreligious, this experience was palatable to me. More than anything else, I was reminded of the many concerts and poetry readings I had attended in college—not so long ago then—nearly all of which had been held in churches. Nothing was required of me. No pledges. No promises. Only aesthetic appreciation.

Not everyone in the congregation approved of Homer Teach's ecumenism as much as I did. The time for Homer's retirement loomed, and the parish's prevailing sentiment was that the call needed to go to someone a little more focused than he had been. It was into this climate that somehow I found myself—a nonreligious, non-believing, poetry-loving person—a member of the Pulpit Committee, the group of six chosen by the church to conduct a search for the new pastor. Perhaps recognizing an ally in my lack of religiosity, Homer himself had approached me and asked if I would serve. It was a time when I already served officially on several other committees around town. That year I was recording secretary for the yacht club, for the hospital volunteers, for the nursery school. My husband used to say that until I wrote up the minutes, no one knew what had happened in town. I used to say that given my perspective, I had a wonderful opportunity to shape some different community forums myself.

So I was in a committee stance. Why not the church committee too?

I literally had no clear understanding of what a "sacred" burden I was undertaking. That's one kind of naiveté.

The Pulpit Committee met once a week for three hours in a kind of spiritual encounter session. United Church of Christ officials led us through a series of tests articulating our religious beliefs, our expectations for the new pastor, which set standards for the search process. The UCC is a mainline Protestant group formed in 1957 of a union between the General Council of the Christian Congregational Church and the Evangelical and Reformed Church. In New England—where my Pulpit Committee experience took place—there are a lot of Congregational churches (a denomination devoted to self-government by each individual congregation) that are not associated with the UCC, an organization characterized by a more liberal perspective and a commitment to active participation by laypersons.

All of that was new to me. It's amazing how a literary person can "pass" in a situation like this. Looking back, I can see now that some of my fellow committee members questioned my presence there. But that's the thing about religion. It's amorphous and personal: there were people on the committee who could articulate a very deep belief in God; and there were people on the committee who were incapable of putting their faith into words but whose eyes glowed with fervor; and there was me, pulling down enough of the right notes to stay on key. Who could judge the extent or sincerity of any of us? The question no one, including myself, ever asked of me was why. Why would I want to do this? I had never professed a religious interest in my life, and yet not even people who knew me questioned my election to this group.

It was, from the beginning, a secret. I was a secret. What I believed —if I believed—was a secret. Especially from myself. I see that now.

I didn't see it then. As I didn't see a number of the activities I engaged in, the beliefs I espoused, as being so outside myself as to be alien, but so central to my existence as to be necessary. A decade later, Carol Gilligan would write in *In A Different Voice* that the way so many women of my generation went through certain actions "set the stage for a kind of privatization of women's experience … [that] impedes the development of women's political voice and presence in the public world." What I have called naiveté. But at the time, I was absorbed in the process of the Pulpit Committee. I was drawn to the orderliness of it. I liked having my big, blue UCC notebook with all those color-coded tabs labeled "Faith," "Belief," "Spirituality." As if all of the abstract teaching of my college English days had been indexed and codified, knowable at last. And maybe that was part of it: perhaps I thought the Big Secret would finally be revealed to me.

Thoughtful or not, I was jazzed up about my participation in the Pulpit Committee. I was living in the country with two small children, quite isolated. The meetings became the most stimulating part of my life. I came home full of stories, stories I had never heard. I had been among many kinds of people in my life, even by then when I was a young woman, but never people of faith. It was not a factor I even considered. Belief in God had not been one of the tenets of my upbringing. In the bohemian circles of my college years, truth and beauty were the big abstractions. In fact, having lived for some time in the academic world—some of it as a student, some as a faculty wife, and some as a publisher of scholarly journals—I was ill-prepared for the customs of the hinterland, as nearsighted and self-satisfied as I would later find my own grown children to be in their dismissal of the world outside the academy. So there I was on the Pulpit Committee, an out-and-out impostor, maybe even a wolf in sheep's clothing. Except I didn't see it that way. I found it amusing. I didn't deceive anyone. I just never clarified my stance. That was easy to do. Yet I was constantly astounded at the depth and solemnity of my fellow committee members. They really believed in this stuff.

My husband soon tired of all this blather. I could see his eyes glazing over at the dinner table. Almost everyone I knew in this community belonged to the church, and even I knew I shouldn't talk to them about the workings of the Pulpit Committee, which were if not secret, inherently "confidential." But I had a neighbor who did not belong to this or any church. When you live in the country, a neighbor is the person who lives the closest to you. Creighton and Elizabeth Thomas lived across the road and half a mile away. Creighton was a boat builder who worked out of a shed behind his house. Several years earlier, my husband and I had built a sailing dingy from scratch—actually from lumber we milled ourselves on our property—so we had a number of specialized woodworking tools, corner chisels, tapered drill bits. Creighton regularly borrowed our tools.

At the time I was on the Pulpit Committee, Creighton was often in and out of our house. Many afternoons he came over to return or exchange tools. We'd have a cup of tea and talk. Creighton was a big, burly man who looked like one of the Smith Brothers on the cough drop box: full-bearded, always dressed in huge bib overalls and a plaid shirt. There was a soft sweetness about Creighton in those days. We talked as neighbors do about our gardens, the weather, goings-on around town. But just as often we talked about publishing and living in Connecticut. I had come to this place out of the academic publishing world in Connecticut, and Creighton had come from Connecticut to be the first editor of a specialty boating magazine.

A slick publication devoted to all aspects of wooden boat owning, building, and history started by a couple of hippies from away, in a barn down the road, the magazine was a local success story. It had gained a national readership within the first year and soon became an institution unto itself: the publication, a boat-building school, retreats, and workshops.

Creighton's editorship helped shape the initial direction of the magazine, but he had differences with the publishers—trust-fund babies from California—and left after the first year. The magazine may not have worked for him, but his interest in boats and coastal living did. He stayed and went to work for himself, first building his own house in the woods and then his specialty, Adirondack rowing sculls, each magnificently wrought. Creighton was apparently something of a trust-fund baby himself, although of a different, more conservative ilk. All I knew was that he had sufficient private income to be able to dabble with his life. As it turned out, there was a great deal I did not know about Creighton Thomas.

Some days I went over to watch the progress on the boat he was building, and to visit with his wife Elizabeth, who was housebound with a new baby. She and I stood amidst aromatic wood shavings in the shed, watching Creighton work. I loved seeing the twenty-foot boats take shape. Boats aren't built like tables or chairs. Boats have special requirements of sheer and draft, the exact meeting of curved lines at particular points that make the construction a marriage of geometry and craftsmanship. A boat builder carries an idea in his head much the same as a sculptor does of an object to be released from earth's dull bounds. There are many methods employed in boat building, but nearly all of them involve a process called "lofting," which consists of drawing the shape of the hull full size on a flat surface.

The boat builder must first have an accurate plan from which he extrapolates longitudinal and diagonal lines—an "offset" table reproducing the curvature—accurately transferring the scale of the plan into real size on a single plane. A lofted plan is usually studded with tiny brad nails, connected by pieces of string until the design of the boat emerges like a huge cat's cradle half model before you.

Creighton often built the same model, but he was a perfectionist and always took down his lofting from the previous one and cast it again when he started a new boat. It's an exciting stage of boat building, when the mold has been set and the planks and battens are cut, waiting for the ribs to fill out the space, similar to how the shape of sculpture begins to emerge from the stone, like those half-finished figures reaching out of blocks that line the Academy hall leading to Michelangelo's *David*.

Creighton was halfway through lofting one afternoon when Elizabeth and I came into the shed. His back was to us as he worked on the wall on the far side from the door.

"I think this is the part I like best," he said without turning. "When I take a measurement and it actually connects in the right place to the one before it! Lord, but it would be wonderful if life could be like that! A string on a wall that showed you exactly where to go and when you would get there!" He turned then, smiling.

Elizabeth was absently sweeping up curls of wood. "Creighton loves 'messing about in boats,' " she said.

"Wrong reference." Creighton corrected her mildly. " 'Messing about in boats' has to do with the water, with rowing and sailing and puttering from place to place. You know me. I never go near the water. I just like to build boats so other people can."

"That's really odd," I said. "I don't think I know a single person whose interest in boats doesn't involve actually getting in one and going on the water."

"Well, you do now," Creighton replied. "What I like about boats is their enormous capacity to occupy space in a certain way. I like the idea of boats. But I have no interest in participating in that idea as it plays itself out."

"That's why you like lofting best," I said. "The idea of the boat measured out on the wall is actually more engaging for you than the boat itself."

"I think you're right," Creighton answered slowly, turning a spindle of twine in his big hands as he stood between the bare spine of his boat and the design on the wall behind him. "Maybe that's a metaphor for how we live."

Another afternoon Creighton and I were sitting in my living room drinking tea and talking about how different our lives were from the ones we had led in Connecticut. I knew he had gone to Yale, and asked him what he had studied.

"Well, undergraduate, I was a history major," he answered, settling into my couch with his big work boots up on a table before him, "but afterwards I went to Divinity School."

"Really?" I nearly dropped my teacup. "I didn't know that—and I never would have guessed it."

He laughed. "Well, it didn't exactly work out, so that's probably why you don't see any traces."

"Where did you go?"

"Oh, I stayed at Yale like my father and grandfather before me. They were both Congregational ministers so I thought probably I ought to be as well." He shook his head and sipped his tea, his big hand holding the fragile handle delicately, easily. Very Yale-like.

"I liked studying theology, but I thought the UCC was becoming too liberal. Too little scriptural emphasis. Too much lay involvement." He sighed. "I was full of myself, thought I could change the world, you know." He gestured to include the room. "I took a calling to a small ghetto church in New Haven …"

I laughed. "I didn't know there were any UCC *ghetto* churches," I interrupted him.

"Oh yes. New Haven is quite a diverse town. It's the original 'town-and-gown' town."

"Well yes, I know about New Haven, but I didn't think the UCC was tending to that particular flock."

"Actually you're right about that. It was my idea. I initiated this parish in a bad part of town. It was a big mistake. All kinds of politics. I realized I didn't have whatever it took to go into a situation like that and lead people up and out." He was looking into his teacup now. "So, well, I started looking around for something else and along came the wooden boats." He smiled. "And here we are."

"And you don't even go to church now, do you?" I asked.

"No, I don't," he answered. "I haven't set foot in a church in ten years, not since I walked out of my own in New Haven."

I had found my audience. For the next two months, I regaled Creighton Thomas with the workings and machinations of the Pulpit Committee. An insider, he could appreciate the subtle changes among the members as we defined and refined the qualities of the perfect pastor for the church. I shared details of résumés with him, who we liked, who we didn't, and why. At this point in the process, we were going around to other Congregational churches in the state in order to hear candidates preach. You do this to preserve the "secrecy" of the selection. A designated church offers its pulpit, makes an announcement that its pastor is away and a guest minister will be preaching. Embedded in the congregation, the Pulpit Committee gets to see the candidate in action. We had already eliminated six or seven people in this way, and it was beginning to look as though our job was not as easy as it had at first appeared.

And the reality of my own situation was sinking in. It was one thing to feel expansive and walk down the red carpet in Homer Teach's transcendental world, quite another to traipse from church to church and listen to endless, boring sermonizing. I liked the idea of being chosen, of being an insider on the Pulpit Committee. I liked my big blue notebook with all the answers. I did not like choosing a pastor. I did not like church. Talking to Creighton was a way for me to keep from thinking about that—and its repercussions—as I dramatized the process for him. Oh, it was shameless. I was like Scheherazade, weaving amusing tales at her master's feet as he sipped tea and threw his big head back and roared at the absurdity of it all. We were co-conspirators, Creighton and I. In this pristine backwater where people actually seemed to live by clichés both he and I would have chopped right out of our Connecticut lives, we reinforced each other's approval and solace by laughing out loud at their expense.

Then it happened. One fresh Sunday morning in April, just after Easter, a strong and definitely different voice lifted up from the choir loft behind me. I looked over my shoulder. There, at the end of the second row, right in the middle of the basses was Creighton Thomas, beard trimmed, wearing quite a nice three-piece suit, balancing his hymnal in one big hand before him as his "Gloria" rang out. I shriveled into my pew. I felt sure the entire congregation was witness to my betrayal.

Did I mention he was charming? At the fellowship hour after

church, he came right over to me and took my hand in both of his, you know, the way preachers do?

"I guess you converted me," he laughed. I laughed too, but all I could think of was that he knew too much about the Pulpit Committee to become a member of this church. I was ashamed. I had broken the trust of the committee. I had indulged myself. And he knew that about me. I said nothing.

He didn't come around for tea again. He didn't need to. Two weeks after I saw him in the choir, Homer Teach introduced Creighton and his family as new members of the parish. Homer beamed to have garnered such a fine addition. Two weeks later, the chairman of the Pulpit Committee announced we had received a late application he thought we should consider, the former Rev. Creighton Thomas. My hands were like ice. That was the moment I might have, to use the relevant vernacular, redeemed myself. It should have been so easy for me to say, "You know, Creighton is a neighbor of mine and we've talked a little about this process …" It should have been possible for me to alert the committee, maybe even save my own face. I said nothing.

Two weeks after that, we went to the Congo Church in the next town to hear Creighton preach. He was brilliant, resonant, commanding, hitting all his marks, thanks to the perfect coaching he had received from me as to what the committee did not like to hear. Sermons are curious. In Divinity School, the course teaching them is called homiletics, after the Greek *homilētikē*, the art of conversation— so much friendlier than "sermon," which comes from the Old French, *sermoner*, to preach. The traditional advice when teaching clergy how to perform the little talk that occurs in the middle of a Christian church service is to relate it to the *pericope*—a passage of scripture read—and then to daily life. For instance, if the reading has been Matthew 14:13-21, the miracle of Jesus sharing five loaves and two fish among the multitude, the homily can be about faith in the face of hunger and then a segue to the parish soup kitchen. We had heard many such formulaic sermons, and while I had summarized some of the worst for Creighton, I suspect that he didn't need my insights to come up with something both different and more enlightening. When his turn came, Creighton spoke about lofting.

That Sunday was Pentecost, the celebration in the Christian world of the inauguration of the Church by the Holy Spirit, the feast day that lends its name to those Johannine believers likewise possessed. The scripture is full of promise, joy, and confirmation of the Way. Church doctrine allows a selection from among several readings. Creighton chose Ezekiel 37:1-14, in which the prophet envisions "dry bones," and then predicts "new life" for the nation of Israel. Creighton gave it cursory due, but the congregation was truly transported when he drew the comparison between the lofting lines that shape and steady a boat being built and the sureness of the Christian path, just as possible to be evenly mapped out on the wall of our lives, just as palpable as Ezekiel's bones. Of course, he got the job. Everyone was so pleased that not only had we found the perfect pastor but he was one of our own.

Well, recently one of our own.

Creighton Thomas and I never talked about the Pulpit Committee or about what I saw as our transgressions, or about anything else, for many years. He busied himself with the parish, and even though he still lived just down the road—choosing to stay in his own home rather than move to the parsonage—we saw little of each other.

When we met, it was cordial, but in reality, I avoided him. Six months into his ministry, I wasn't even going to church anymore. That place seemed tainted to me now, the setting for my mortification. Even more tainted was my notion of myself. I had been given a serious responsibility and I had treated it like a joke. It didn't matter that I didn't believe in those things—of course, if I had been honest, I would never have accepted the appointment in the first place—what mattered was that I had betrayed that trust, I had undermined the process, and I had turned the whole endeavor into a parody of itself. I didn't like what that showed me about myself.

You may ask what does that matter. If Creighton wanted the job, if the congregation was pleased with him, then you could even say God works in mysterious ways, his wonders to perform. Couldn't you? I mean you could if you were one of those people who believed in God and his wonders. And wasn't that the point too? That these people did and I had no business muddling among them. Someone else may have been able to see me as the unwitting instrument of God's will, but I didn't see myself that way. And that was the point too. Whatever else I believed, I did believe that Creighton Thomas was like me. I believed that he and I shared the same deep secret: that we represented ourselves as embracing beliefs we did not hold; that we were each guilty of the sin of pride. And there were two of us who knew that the working out of the Pulpit Committee was not God's will, but rather, Creighton Thomas', and more, he had contrived to manipulate it and used me to that end. We each said nothing.

It was Creighton Thomas' willfulness that did him in. That's the *hubris* part. Within a year of his taking the position, rumblings began in the congregation. Whereas Homer Teach's sermons were a little too lyrical and transcendental, Creighton's were a little too literal and fundamentalist. Once he donned those robes and stood up front in that beautiful old church, Creighton assumed the hard and judgmental stance that had been living all along inside him. He even seemed to grow larger. He stood taller. His beard filled out. His strong bass rolled off the back pews. Before long there was whispering in town about prayer groups speaking in tongues, about harshness with the children in Sunday school, about literal interpretations of the scripture. After the first few weeks, there were no more felicitous homilies about boat building and the Lord: there were sermons about the wrath of God being brought down hard on all who strayed. The explicatory attention he had shown to the whole scripture at Pentecost was replaced long before Advent by scrutiny of a single verse, isolated, exacting, and conservative.

The deacons took Creighton aside and cautioned him to lighten up. He rose to his full height, thrust out his considerable chest, and took great umbrage. The choir was reduced to two pieces per service, approved by him; the sermons stretched to double length. The UCC elders came from Connecticut to remind him of the charter, of the uniformity of the concordance and its differences from the more "literal" brethren. The original flock fell away. There were some new converts from over at the Baptist church on Pleasant Street.

But some of the original congregation would not relinquish their pulpit to this interloper. In the end, Creighton Thomas became the first pastor of the Congregational Church in that town to be asked to leave—by means of a public vote—in its two-hundred-year history. I attended that meeting, way in the back, watched the anger and arrogance in Creighton's unyielding posture. I did not vote. I did not feel I had the right. I felt responsible for bringing this situation to pass.

I felt that if I had not painted such pictures in Creighton's head on those sunlit afternoons in my living room, all of this darkness would not have come down upon these innocent people. Talk about *hubris*.

That's what happens with secrets. It's so delicious to have them. But they get out of hand. They make you do things you wouldn't even have considered doing, as I had to the professor in Starbucks. They make you capricious and willful. I don't believe Creighton Thomas really wanted to be pastor of the Congregational Church. I believe he became inflamed by my secrets. I believe he did it because he could. I believe I offered him a vision of himself, and that like lofting a boat, Creighton cast the lines of his life upon the wall of his mind and lifted up off my couch to begin an abstract, strung-out journey into the dark spirit hidden within him. And I believe he acted in secret even from himself.

The same year that Creighton was removed from the church, I left that town and the threads of this story were lost to me. Then, twenty years later—not long after I sing-songed the professor—I returned for a friend's funeral. Creighton Thomas was at the viewing, an itinerant pastor now to several fundamentalist churches around the county. He had grown even larger, but also a little down-at-heel. There was a seediness about his dress, his thinning hair, and the set of his jaw. He looked hard.

He came right over to me and took my hand between both of his, you know, the way preachers do?

"You've changed," he said, leaning to look me in the eyes. I felt like a moth pinned to a board. I felt caught out.

"Well, a little older, a little wiser," I managed. "We've all changed, haven't we?"

"I think I'm constant," Creighton answered, still holding my hand between his own.

"That's a curious word." I tried to laugh. "I don't think of it as describing our lives. It's more a matter of the heart."

"Exactly," Creighton said, finally letting go of my hand. I nearly reeled away from him. He smiled thinly. "That's my secret."

I thought then, as I had so often over the years, of Creighton in his boat-building shed. I pictured him standing in his bib overalls among the wood shavings, running those same big hands tenderly over the lofting on his wall. The strings in both our lives had tangled considerably since that day. I had moved far away. Our children were grown. Creighton had lost his church but strengthened in his faith. He harbored now an utter conviction of the rightness of his way and the extreme application of scripture. Elizabeth was bent and silenced. There were no more boats being built.

It occurred to me that perhaps Creighton felt about religion the same as he felt about boats, that he liked the idea but not the way it played itself out. Perhaps he had truly lost his way on that abstract spiritual ocean. Perhaps he should have stayed as dry with the church as he had with his boats.

"Do you ever give your lofting sermon?" I asked him then as we stood before my friend's coffin.

"Lofting?" He looked puzzled.

"Yes, remember the sermon you preached for the Pulpit Committee?"

Creighton laughed outright, looking for an instant like the man he had been when I first met him.

"Oh Lord. That one. Yeah, I remember. And no, I haven't given it. That was a Homer Teach sermon. I thought you'd all eat it up." I was shocked at his cynicism.

"You mean you didn't feel that way about lofting?" I asked, unable to let it go.

"Sure I felt that way about lofting," Creighton answered, beginning to look over my head and around the room, ready to move on. "I just don't feel that way about the Lord. You take care now. Good to see you."

He walked past me then and clasped someone else's hand between both of his. I turned. Across his broad back I imagined a cat's cradle of twine strung, all those desires spinning out to the end, all those designs fastened to infinity. My secret life incarnate.

Swiftwater

We were reading *Swiftwater* by Paul Annixter in my eighth-grade Opportunity class the day Jake Fuller shot a deer from my classroom window. It was November, the beginning of the gray motionless light that would cover upstate New York until at least Memorial Day. By second period, nine to ten, all the brightness of the day already filled the sky. Inside, the classroom took on a pearly luminescence, especially soft near the windows, growing less definite as it penetrated across the room. A month later, the wane began by lunchtime, and every afternoon from December through March, I switched on the overheads. We didn't know about seasonal affective disorder in those days—or at least I didn't—but when I think back now on that time in St. Lawrence County, there is a definite SAD feeling to the experience, a deprivation of nurture, enlightenment.

Even though this was an eighth-grade class, most of the kids were at least two years older than grade age. Jake, I think, was sixteen. They liked *Swiftwater*. A year later, in 1965, it would be made into a Disney movie called *Those Calloways,* which always puzzled me because *Swiftwater* is such a pristine title, evoking as it does both action and cleansing. The book is about a family trying to build a geese sanctuary in rural Maine. Cam Calloway, the father, moves them further and further into the woods in hope of buying a lake to protect the migratory birds, and also to preserve old-fashioned vigor and values. Although I never saw the movie, I gathered from promotional pictures that the Calloways had been transformed into "pretty" rustics. But that devaluation hadn't taken place yet when we were reading *Swiftwater* in the fall of 1964. My class loved all the ice chipping and water lugging, the rigors of country life not so very much removed from their own situations.

They were especially taken by the adolescent son, Bucky, and his encounter with a wolverine on his trap line. Trapping was something my students understood. Although I grew up in a family that hunted and fished, we were not trappers. I don't think it was ideological. Maybe fastidiousness. All that skinning and scraping on the inside. But these upstate New York kids, even the girls, all ran trap lines. They were full of stories about foxes and mink and weasels, fishers, marten, muskrat, furry pelts they regularly delivered to an agent in Massena on the Seaway who bought the skins for less than a dollar each, then took them upriver to Montreal, only an hour away, where furriers snipped and sewed them into the linings of mittens, hats, boots. Not one of my students owned a fur-lined garment, but they all knew exactly how their wares had been used, as well as the validity of the trapping practice. "There are fourteen species of fur-bearing animals in New York State," they quoted to me out of the regulation manual—these kids who could scarcely read from *Dick and Jane*—"and their populations are abundant and secure."

In *Swiftwater*, Bucky's trap line takes him deep into the interior, where he is hoping for red fox. The family's ability to purchase a lake for the geese is tied to the success of their trapping, so this storyline is key. A trap line has to be checked (by law) every twenty-four hours to make sure the trap hasn't been sprung—"grinned" is the expression a trapper uses—or that an animal isn't suffering. Even underage-for-hunting trappers are allowed to carry firearms, for killing a trapped animal is sanctioned by "any means under the law" during any season. Cam wouldn't let Bucky carry a gun so he ran his line with a short-sawed club tucked into his back pocket for the swift dispatch of his catches. Trapping occurs in the winter when the pelt is thick, and not in spring or summer when the animals may be tending to young; Bucky has to plow through a lot of deep snow to run his lines. He's just extricated himself from a drift and is trying to catch his breath on the edge of an ice cliff when the wolverine corners him.

The wolverine is truly a wretched animal. I can't imagine how they came to be endangered. No one hunts them except humans (for their fur) and they live in such desolate, frigid, northern regions, there is scarcely anyone around to do that. The wolverine is the largest land-dwelling member of the *Mustelidae* genus (minks, otters, skunks, weasels). If a wolverine were the size of a bear rather than the size of a Shetland sheepdog, it would be the strongest animal on earth, for it possesses enormous jaw strength and tenacity, the only animal of its size (thirty-six pounds) to regularly kill deer, caribou, and moose.

No one in my class had ever seen a wolverine—although its range extended to the very schoolyard door—nor heard of anyone who had. They all expected I knew them well since I'd gone to a school where the sports team was called the Wolverines. My only experience with the animal was the stuffed one behind glass in a diorama on the second floor of the natural science building on the campus in Ann Arbor. That wolverine looks ferocious: rearing up flat-footed on its hind legs like a bear, jaws open wide and all thirty-eight razor-sharp teeth shining, all ten claws extended, curved and threatening. Blood drips down its pelt as it defends a dead deer at its feet on the frozen tundra of the Upper Peninsula. The northern lights blaze overhead.

Based on this exposure, I was prepared to agree that Bucky's situation was serious.

I was reading that section out loud to the class. Sometimes I called upon them to read a few sentences, but we'd let that go, since the pace slowed down as a student stumbled through the text. Gradually, "Reading Time" had become "Story Time." We were all into *Swiftwater*. I was on the window side of the classroom, my back to the glass, up near the front. I was leaning against the sill, holding the book out before me, lost with Bucky in the snow, confronting the snarling wolverine. Seven rows of desks facing the blackboard at the front, to my left, spread out before me. Probably I was leaning a little to the left myself, because I never saw Jake Fuller get up out of his seat, last in the second row away from the windows. I never saw him pick up the rifle lying under some coats at the back of the room behind his desk. I never heard the window crank when he dropped the bottom pane open. I never saw the gun steadied on the edge of the frame.

Bucky turned and the wolverine howled when the gun went off—BANG! At first I thought it was Cam to the rescue. My captive students, cocooned inside the smoky light, exploded. What I remember now are all the colors. Eunice Roach's red sweater. Roy Brickle's yellow shirt. Jake Fuller's green jacket. Blue *Swiftwater* books on all the desks. Colors bright and primary bleeding into our muted world. Everyone ran to the windows. There on the snow, just beyond the goal posts, lay a dead buck, front legs tucked under its chest, a pink flower blossoming beneath it.

"Holy shit, Jake!" Roy Brickle said. "Look's like a six-pointer."
I want to say they high-fived, but I don't think people high-fived yet in 1964. But it was a high-five moment. Suddenly, I smelled the acrid gun powder. A puff of smoke in the room dissipated in the steely light.

Jake was standing by the window, looking down at the buck, the rifle cradled in his right arm.

"Jake!" I cried, pushing through the kids to him. "Give me that gun." He looked surprised but handed it over without a word. I remember the heft of that gun. I remember that it was warm, not cold the way I think of guns, because when I've used guns myself, it's been outside, and usually, it's been outside in fall or winter so the gun is cold, so cold it makes your bare hands hurt. I remember how warm that gun was. An inside gun.

People always ask me when I tell this story, "What did you say?" I have no idea. I don't remember what I said. I don't remember what anyone said, except I remember Roy Brickle said it looked like a six-pointer and I know I asked Jake for the gun. Bucky and the wolverine and Jake Fuller and the dead deer and the warm gun are all living in the same place inside my head. Everything else is far away, distant and unreal in the silver light.

Outside our window, figures streamed across the snow toward the dead deer. Teachers, students, cooks from the cafeteria. Figures sharp and prominent cutting through the monochromatic day, parting the dense air around them. Superintendent John McKay reached the carcass first. He knelt down by the deer and then stood and looked back at the school, scanning the second-floor windows. How like that moment when someone saw a rifle nosing out of the Texas School Book Depository barely a year earlier. Time telescoped for me and it seemed as though John McKay was standing on the grassy knoll, one of those instances when one image superimposes over another, blurring all the edges, and I could be Lee Harvey Oswald. I was standing up close to the window, the rifle butt in my right hand, its body nestled alongside my breast. John's eyes met mine.

At that moment, Bonnie Slater touched my shoulder from behind. "What in hell is going on?" she said in my ear. I turned to see my classroom full, her students, my students, kids from all up and down the corridor squeezing in to congratulate Jake Fuller.

"I thought maybe you plugged John McKay," Bonnie said, her blue eyes twinkling. "Oh my Lord. Can you believe this?"

"Class!" I called, regaining teacher stance. "In your seats!"

"Oh, come on," Schuyler said from the doorway. He'd come all the way up from his chemistry lab. "This is big stuff. What'd you get, Jake? A buck?"

"Yes sir, Mr. Olsen," Jake answered. "Roy says it might be a six-pointer." Schuyler elbowed into the window space and looked out. It was hard to tell, since so many people were standing now around the dead deer.

"Good size," he allowed.

Just then John McKay burst through my door. "Don't tell me you got that buck?" he yelled. I was still holding the gun.

"No, no, Mr. McKay," I said. "I just took the rifle away from a student. I was ..."

"Who? Who got that deer?"

"I did, sir. I got him," Jake said, stepping away from the crowd around the window.

"Well I'll be damned," John said, striding over to Jake and clapping him on the shoulder. "Didn't think you had balls enough for something like that, Fuller. Good man!" He turned then and made a sweeping gesture around the room. "Assembly. Five minutes. Get your butts in gear!" And he was out the door.

Schuyler chuckled and started pushing kids toward the corridor. He looked back at Bonnie and me, both of us now leaning against the window sill. He walked over and took the rifle out of my hand. "Doesn't go with your hair," he said, and walked out the door with the gun slung over his shoulder.

The assembly John McKay called to reward Jake Fuller for shooting a deer from my classroom window was, in retrospect, not the most surprising thing that happened in the sixties. I didn't tell this story for a long time because I wasn't sure how I felt about it. After I left upstate New York three years later to return to Ann Arbor, in August of 1967, driving through the safe Canadian farmland and over the bridge at Windsor into Detroit, burning in the riots that marked those days, it was as though the flames of the times, the red light reflecting off the buildings on Eight Mile Road, sucked up all the gray light and life of my experience in the St. Lawrence valley, pushing it back into a hidden place in my mind at a time in the world when we were already becoming inured to the sound of gunfire in unlikely places. So, I forgot. I forgot the school. I forgot the dull light. I forgot Jake Fuller and John McKay.

But there was something sweet about that day. Something pure. Jake Fuller acted entirely out of instinct. The clarity and economy of not only Jake's action but the school community's response to it impressed me. It was what it was. I like to think it's because I'm a reader and because the whole incident, for me, got mixed up with *Swiftwater*. When I thought about Jake and the deer, I always thought about Bucky and the wolverine. When I talked about Jake's family sharing some of the venison with the school for a special luncheon, I was always picturing those Calloways and wondering how the geese sanctuary worked out. I've spent years mixing up life with art.

John McKay had Jake's buck's head mounted to hang in his office at school. Roy was right. It was a six-pointer. John had a little brass plaque installed on the curved wooden mount: "November 18, 1964. Jacob Fuller." Nearly forty years later, the deer's head has migrated to near the trophy case in the hall outside John's old office, right between that and the veterans' memorial. Another plaque has been installed under the original: "Jacob Fuller: 1948 – 1972. Killed in Vietnam."

All Hands

I'm taking my father deep-sea fishing off the coast of Maine. He'll be eighty soon and had a stroke last fall. He was raking leaves in his back yard in Michigan when he pitched face down into a pile of silver maple. A physical, vigorous man who was once a Golden Gloves champion and always a first-class fisherman, he is now, nine months after the event, "rehabilitated" to a confused, shuffling old man, plucking at his clothes and looking around wildly.

Down in the Florida Keys last winter where the high sun and sweet breezes healed him a little, he was without his boat for the first time in twenty years. For the first time in twenty years he couldn't go fishing every day. For the first time in twenty years he didn't spend his afternoons filleting snapper, gangling pelicans diving all around him.

Some fellow fishermen volunteered to take him out, but he scared the wits out of them, fumbling with his lines, losing his balance. In response, he succumbed to the numb anger of the speechless when their faculties desert them.

"They didn't want to take me out because I'm a cripple," he tells me on the dock this morning, recounting last winter's failure and wiping tears from his eyes, spittle gathering in the corners of his mouth. "I can still catch a lot of good fish." His once full mouth is drawn now, his bottom lip shiny, stretched sleek and pink as a fish's underjaw.

So here we are at seven on an August morning in Maine, waiting on the wharf in Portland for the skipper of the *Indian Days*, a battered tub of a boat with blood-stained plywood nailed over the seats, beards of algae drooping from her dock lines. Dad is looking over the rail down to the dock below where the *Indian Days* is riding next to a ramshackle collection of plastic crates with letters and numbers taped in silver on their sides.

"Looks good," he says, and I look again myself to see what might have prompted that judgment. Our fellow fishermen appear seasoned. They're laden with Playmate coolers and plastic bags full of sweatshirts and oilskins. No sports here. They're dressed like mechanics in greasy denim and Red Sox hats, a few kids in rude tee shirts and very big shoes. There is one other woman besides myself, a hard blond with braids and neon green barrettes, a bright yellow halter top, pack of Newports nestling next to her shades in the cleavage. Fifty if she's a day.

"Hey," she greets me. "I'm Trudy. Don't you just love this?"

Actually, I do. I love the ocean and I love to fish, although I don't do much of it these days. When I was a child, the only relationship I ever had with my father was forged while fishing. Every summer, the "Kids," as my parents were called by their parents, would drive the four hundred miles "up north" to the western edge of Michigan's mitten to visit me where I was snugged down at the top of the ring finger in relative comfort, living with my maternal grandparents.

Years later I would say my parents had abandoned me to my grandparents after putting me on a bus at age three in Waco, Texas, dressed in a white pinafore with a note pinned to the ruffle asking folks to look out for me on the two-week trip to Michigan. It was 1943; the world was at war. My father was flying B-25s for the Army Air Corps, and my mother wanted to dance and play pool at the officers' club. Family legend has it that I sang and entertained passengers all across the country. I wonder how they knew that? I repeated this story proudly for years until it occurred to me to be angry. But that was much later.

Those dusky summer evenings when the Kids rolled into my grandparents' small dull town in their convertible, beautiful and exotic—my mother with her bright red lipstick and cigarettes, my father, muscular and grinning, a long-necked beer in one hand— I felt neither angry nor abandoned. It was as if Hedy Lamarr and Van Johnson had come to town, and for that brief week of their summer vacation every year, I belonged to the Kids. I was part of the romance.

And my father took me fishing.

The skipper of the *Indian Days* is giving a speech about etiquette aboard his vessel: no swearing; no alcohol or drugs; share the rail. There is a lot of grinning and nudging amongst our fellow fishermen, many of whom are clasping six-packs to their chests and who knows what else inside those bags. I ask if my father and I can have early boarding since I see it's going to take quite a while to get him down that ramp and along the landing to the boat. There is a groan. My father, speechless, glares at me. The skipper says, sure, come along, but we find ourselves left behind in the rush as the rest of the group, not a rail sharer among them, clambers down the ramp to board the *Indian Days*.

The ramp is a narrow strip of plywood with wooden stops at intervals, railings, and rollers on the bottom to allow it to ride down when the tide is high, roll back when the tide is low. Right now it's dead low, so we're at a steep incline. I stand in front of my father as he makes his way down the stops. His arms are still muscular.

His big hands are quivering, stretched tight white as he holds himself upright on the railings.

It takes forever. I can feel impatience rising from fifteen feet below us on the boat. Fishermen like to get going. We gain the landing and begin to negotiate the final twenty-five feet. Even though the morning is calm, the floating dock rides with the roll of passing traffic and the incoming tide. It's about ten feet wide, but as my father lurches along, I am terrified he will plunge into the oily darkness under the wharf and rise to float like debris among the pilings. I clench my teeth and try to seem nonchalant. Good going, Dad! Why does infirmity in others bring out the imbecility in ourselves? The skipper doesn't have these problems. He strides on ahead and hops aboard.

Aboard is not an easy maneuver. The gunwales are at least three feet above the landing, another three feet down to the deck of the boat. They bring us some makeshift steps, without rails, that push up against the bobbing side of the *Indian Days*. My father balks like a stallion at the gate. If he had a halter, I'd be pulling it. He pushes me aside and gets up the first step, then stops short. The steps are too narrow for another person to stand alongside. I keep smiling. Then, in a swoop, the skipper and his first mate each take one of my father's arms from inside the boat and swing him, kicking, up and over: aboard.

He is furious.

It gets dark late in northern Michigan in the summertime, not until after nine. And dinner, when I was a child, was early, around five thirty, so there was always a long time to play outside before bedtime, even when I was quite young. When I think now of those summer evenings in that tiny town where I spent my childhood with my grandparents, I see it from above, looking down on fewer than a hundred houses nestled in a valley surrounded by cedar swamps. Cedar was the name of the town, and there was cedar everywhere, the airy awls brushing my face as I played hide-and-seek, peeking through its flat reaching fingers, my breath chilled by its redolent aroma. In my memories, there are always fireflies.

And the mitten. Anyone who grows up in Michigan knows the state is shaped like a left-handed mitten, palm facing away. The southeastern part of the state is always called the Thumb: "General showers in the metropolitan Detroit area; snow flurries in the Thumb." When a person gives directions there or wants to show you where he lives, he holds up his left hand and points to wherever the place is. As a child, I always had a sense of being on the mitten, like a pattern superimposed over my experience, at once distancing and locating it. All the years I lived in Cedar, there was a picture in my head of where I was—up at the top of the ring finger—and where the Kids were—just below the Thumb: a thread stitched across the palm connecting us.

I see myself, a sturdy girl with long braids, watching, looking to see if I could discover that special thing keeping the families around me together; what it was we lacked. It was the kind of town and still the time in America where children ran in and out of everyone's houses, where adults felt the responsibility to call out caution or shake a restraining finger at all the children, whoever they belonged to. I could go anywhere. But I belonged nowhere. A convert, I wasn't really Catholic; half-Irish, I wasn't even Polish like everyone else in town. Something was funny. I had no brothers or sisters, and apparently my parents didn't want me. I had some friends, but what I remember about that time is being alone or being with my grandmother.

Everyone in my family describes my grandmother Cecile as a coquette. That's the word they use. As a child I didn't understand that word, but I understood my grandmother was dishonest, I understood that she said one thing and did another. When I lived with her, she was a woman in her fifties and I was only seven. She was overweight, a big woman, but she still carried herself like the tall red-haired beauty who had nursed my grandfather during the influenza epidemic of 1918, and she still fluttered around men, melting like sweet boiled icing into a shape it seemed no one saw but me. I was always watching her, and she was always watching me. I think now she knew that I knew her secrets. I knew that while she said she really wasn't hungry and picked at tiny portions on her plate at the table, earlier she had stuffed herself behind the curtain in the pantry.

Cecile dressed her long white hair up into a chignon with two wings sweeping away from her high, broad forehead. Everyday she laced herself into a full corset and put on a starched "housedress," a cotton one-piece garment with three-quarter sleeves and a square neckline that buttoned all the length of its center front. She powdered her pink cheeks white and painted her pale lips pink; her eyes were china blue and vacant, reflecting the judgment she passed on the world: cool, crazy. She sat in a chair at the dining room window, behind lace curtains, and watched the town move around her. She hardly ever went out, so everyone came to her. Cecile thought she was too good for the people of Cedar. She thought my mother was too good for my father. She guessed I would go the same way, ruined by sex and men. When I got old enough, I ran out into the cedar trees to escape her; before then, I hid in the house.

There was an oval library table in the living room with carved legs curling out from the four rounded corners, a shelf underneath for magazines. When I was small, I took the magazines carefully off the shelf and stacked them neatly on the floor. Then I sat on that shelf, hidden, safe, under the table. I sat there for hours, often doing nothing, just listening to the sounds of the house. Sometimes I colored. Sometimes I listened to *The Jungle Book* on shiny 78s my Aunt Betty kept under the wooden wind-up Victrola, loving Shere Khan, the tiger, and humming along with Kaa, the python. The big cardboard box holding the records had pictures of Sabu, who played Mowgli in the movie, riding an elephant, and pictures of Bagheera, the panther, stalking in high grass. I examined those pictures over and over, bewitched by a world where a boy whose parents had lost him, as my parents had lost me, could be rescued by wolves. It gave me hope. It made me love animals.

I have that table in my own living room now. Recently when I was polishing the wood, I leaned under it to take my own magazines off the shelf. I stacked them neatly on the floor and was shocked to be put back by the gesture to that place where I had been as a child in my grandmother's house, curled up under this table. The shelf seemed so small. I leaned into the space, my hands on the flat surface. I looked up to the underside of the table top. In the corner was printed "Penny loves Mommy Phyl" in a child's red crayon.

Mommy Phyl. Phyllis, my absent parent who never wanted to be called by any of the names that sounded like Mother; who signed letters to her only child far away, "Love from Mommy Phyl." Mommy Phyl who insists now, sixty years later, that she be called "Mamán," a name foreign enough, perhaps, to absorb the onus. "Mamán," who never let my children, her only grandchildren, call her Grammy or Grandma but insisted upon "Nana." Nana who, at eighty-three, says "Don't call me 'Mrs. Carnahan,' it makes me sound so old." Phyllis, Mommy Phyl, "Mamán," Nana: one of the Kids.

The *Indian Days* heads west out of the harbor, out through the channel past Portland Head Light, where this particular morning thousands of people are gathered on the rocks awaiting the finish of the Beach-to-Beacon road race. They appear to us as a multitude exalting at the base of the lighthouse, suppliants, perhaps, in some ritual of the sea. My father and I have taken up a place in the stern, sitting on a bulkhead centered about two feet forward of the transom. A big green spray froths away from the twin screws right under where we're sitting. The noise renders conversation moot. As we sit silently in the roar, the ruddy red-bricked city of Portland falls away behind us, that broad sinking curve only seen at sea; the obverse of Atlantis rising.

The throng around the lighthouse soon diminishes into monochromism, for the ocean reduces everything touching it to liquidity, blurring and softening the landscape to its own gray-green hues. Soon our gaze has shifted to the rising and falling swells, and we begin the acclimation that occurs when a vessel sails out of sight of land, that twofold sensation of feeling incredibly isolated while at the same time being at the center of our own world on the boat.

We are further isolated when fog cocoons us as we make the turn toward Jericho Ledge. The shining day where runners streak under dappled trees to Portland Head Light is now eclipsed; the sun, a hazy suggestion somewhere high above. The wind turns cool and moist. Wisps of corporeal air curl like smoke off our starboard bow. Collars are turned up. Hands are jammed down hard into dampening pockets. As the sky hunkers down, spirits on board the *Indian Days* buoy up: this is fishing weather.

I spent the summer I was eleven in my grandparents' hot, airless attic, transcribing the *Black Stallion* stories into verse. It was a feverish, painstaking labor, each book translated compulsively intact, strophe after strophe:

> *"But then the Black*
> *Without a look back*
> *Carried Alec away*
> *Far ahead of the Bay."*

I worked in pencil in a child's rough tablet, sitting at a round oak table, bare legs hooked around the big clawed ball feet, sweat soaking my braids. It was something I had to do. The rhythms soothed and calmed me. Years later, when my own daughters attended summer camps, I learned about girls and horses, but it was not something I knew in 1951 when I confused, as I often would, poetry and sex.

My time was drawing near. My grandfather had loved me when I was a little girl. But when I took to wearing short shorts and hanging around the softball field flirting with the players, he wanted me out of his house. I was put on another bus, this time from northern Michigan to southern—from the tip of the ring finger down to below the Thumb of the mitten, a journey pulling through the thread that connected me to the Kids. It must have been hard for my parents to have me arrive on a bus nine years after they'd put me aboard in Texas. It was as though I hadn't existed for all that time while I lived with my grandparents, yearning for the summers when the Kids would visit.

When I think of my father, I am looking up at him. I see his face looming over mine, contorted with rage, puffy, as he bends down, banging my head against the kitchen floor, two big hands cupping my ears. Even parents who live with their children have a hard time with preteens. I was twelve. I hadn't yet realized I should be angry because they put me on that bus in Texas all those years before and then forgot about me in between. I hadn't yet learned to say I'd been abandoned. But I was unhappy about something. I was at home with my grandparents and then I was not. I was wanted and then I was not. I was in and then I was out.

My father and I sat at the kitchen table and screamed at each other.

"You go right back to your room, young lady, and wipe that lipstick off your face."

"I'll wear lipstick if I want to. You can't stop me."

"You're not leaving this house wearing those tight pants."

"I'll wear what I want."

He sat in the corner, an aqua wall behind his head covered with dried drips of running egg yolk, slivers of china embedded in a sprayed pattern like gunshot. I used to regularly throw my breakfast plate at him. He used to regularly jump up and push me to the floor, bang my head, and then stomp out the door. My mother took to her bedroom with a three-year migraine. She must have come out the year I left, at fifteen, to go live with my best friend's parents, just down the road.

I didn't see them then for years. I worked all though high school, worked all through college. I could do what I wanted. I didn't need anyone. And they never came looking for me. Not then. The summer between my sophomore and junior years in college, when I was working at a resort hotel in the Adirondacks, my father showed up, newly divorced from my mother, drunk, ready to be a Kid again. He still looked like Van Johnson then, still had the charm and bouncy off-the-balls-of-his-feet fighter's walk. Still had those big broad hands covered with glowing copper hairs. Still had those thick strong wrists. Just like mine.

I went to get him at his motel, woke him up where he slept on his back, mouth slack. There was just a faint light from the open door behind me. When I shook his shoulder, he turned, reached up and pulled my head down for a kiss. I reared back, but not before I saw his full mouth reaching for mine, not before I saw his eyes look straight into mine as close as when he had me on the kitchen floor.

It takes the *Indian Days* an hour and a half to get out to sea, out to Jericho Ledge where the water is deep enough for cod. We wallow and plow through the fog, rising and falling up and down the troughs of bigger, broader water offshore. I realize we have reached our spot when I see people beginning to rig their gear, getting ready to fish.

My father always brings his own poles, his own special reels and jigs. I help him open up the tackle box, begin to set the rods. People are edging up to the rail and I want to secure our spot. It's hard to get him up. Suddenly, the skipper cuts the engine. The silence is disorienting. The boat maintains its forward momentum for a minute and then turns, nosing up into the wind, broadside to the sea. In the stern, we are pitching in ten-foot swells.

The other fishermen are all business, taking their spots, setting their hooks. I get Dad up and into the port corner of the stern where he has two sides to lean against. It's a prime spot because he can cast off either the side or stern of the boat. I don't meet the eyes of fishermen who had picked out that corner for themselves. There is a lot of talk about bait, who's using what. Cod are found in about two hundred feet of water, moving up and down in a band from the bottom to fifty or seventy-five feet above. It's best to rig a couple of lures at different intervals on heavy-test line, use a multiple-hooked spike on the end and finish it off with a big triangular lead sinker to ensure the line gets down that hundred fifty feet to where the fish are.

My father is fumbling with smaller leaders in his tackle box.

"Here, Dad," I say, "let's use the stainless steel." He glares at me and turns his back, buries a hook in the flesh of his palm.

"Look what you made me do!" He rips the hook out, leaving an ugly jagged slash. I take a BAND-AID out from the box but he has already wrapped a handkerchief around his hand. Blood blossoms through the white cloth across the pad of his thumb. Leaning into the corner as the *Indian Days* takes a hard turn into the freshening breeze, we both watch the stain spread. We don't look at each other. I'm thinking of his anticoagulation medicine. I so want to do the right thing, even after all these years. I don't want him to be hurt on my watch. Whatever may happen to him, I don't want it to happen when he's with me. I would have to deal then with the truth of my intention. I wonder what he's thinking. I'm thinking infection and blood poisoning. I'm thinking serves you right, you willful bastard. Transfixed by his body's process, we both watch the rosy flower fade to pale pink where the handkerchief bends around his thumb.

"We ought to rinse that with some salt water," I say finally, determined to be the good daughter he has never had, the daughter I could never be.

"Doctors," he says, dismissing me, and turns back to the rail. I rig and set his pole beside him. He throws out the line with a recklessness that could have taken off somebody's head. This time I look at the guys on either side and in unison they shrug sympathetically, feet set wide apart, hips snugged up to the rail.

"Hey, Harry," says the one on the port, a biker with a blue bandanna tied around his forehead, "let's do it!"

"Fucking A," my father answers, a crazed, lopsided grin leaping up the good side of his face. "I can still catch a lot of good fish."

But he doesn't. Hours pass and they're pulling them in on either side: big keeper cod, pollock, cusk, even a striped bass. The crew is in action, assigning those numbered plastic crates to each fisherman, taking his catch, cleaning it with a swift knife, and dropping the fish into each's crate along with a shovelful of ice. Entrails slither in fish blood underfoot. As much as I want to, as much as I had looked forward to this rare opportunity, I don't fish at all. So that I can give Dad my full attention, I haven't even rigged a pole. He's making an agitated chewing movement with his mouth, which I recognize as angry gnashing. He is hunched over the rail, elbows on the wood, a stance I know makes it impossible for him to feel any play in his line. I remember then, too, that he doesn't have a lot of feeling left in his right hand. I realize how futile this gesture of mine to take him fishing is. He is not going to catch a lot of good fish. He is not going to catch anything at all.

Then, so fast that I don't even see it happen, the *Indian Days* slaps into a swell, the stern rears up and my father falls flat on his back in the corner, his head hitting the gunwale on the way down with a loud crack. His pole flies up and out, landing in the waves tip first. It is pulled under instantly, straight down, as though there were a fish winning on the other end of the line. His eyes are glassy, unfixed. He can't even look up at me.

My earliest childhood memories are of walking barefoot across wet grass in the dark early morning, feeling with my toes for the night crawlers surfacing after my father's hosing the lawn. Of being hunkered down in the chill bow of an aluminum boat at dawn, putt-putting out with him in the gray half-light. I'm sure my lifelong habit of being an early riser—a trait the world looks upon as virtuous—

was forged in those expeditions of my youth, where getting up and out early had nothing whatsoever to do with virtue. We were gripped instead by that elemental pull of water combined with the possibility of a heart-stopping tug on the line. There is no combination of experiences in nature more exciting than actually being on the water and attached by a thin filament to something—who knew what?—down under the surface. To a child, to this child, there was never a more electric sensation.

Those summer mornings when my father took me fishing in northern Michigan, we trolled for pike and drifted along the farther shores of Lake Leelanaw, casting for largemouth bass. It was a big lake, nearly twenty miles long and five across, reedy down at the southern end. At dawn, its surface was a mirror, streaked by schools of gar, lines drawn across the water, those prehistoric six-foot sliver fish coasting just under the surface in only a few feet of water. My father would ease among them in the shallows with the motor off. I remember kneeling on the bow of the boat, pushing apart the grassy reeds, and looking down at the gar on either side. They moved effortlessly with a slow flick of their dorsal fins, set far back just before the tail, intent, it seemed to me, on some journey that may have started centuries before. It was like being able to see dinosaurs, looking down on those ancient fish. It was our secret world.

Later in the day, we could always catch our limit of sunfish, bluegills, and rock bass down among the submerged stumps in shallow water at the mouth of the Cedar River. This was my favorite kind of fishing, being able to look down and actually see a fish nibbling at my hook! And sometimes we would head up the river, dreamily, as though we were responding to its power and had been drawn by the current's tug into a tunnel of dark water through bulrushes as far as the eye could see. Here the water stopped flowing and pulled instead at the long tops of lank weeds just below the surface. The oars dipped little splashes, eddies pushing the grasses down and away. Pond turtles, round black ovals with red and green jeweled necks, sat in lines on logs charred by lightning fires. They plopped one by one into the water and sank below us into the dark.

Once I reached out and pulled up the fat root of a water hyacinth, those heady, fragrant floating lilies. Wrapped around it was a thick black water snake. What world was this? Who knew what might be down there? I don't remember a single word my father spoke when we were fishing, but I remember everything about the magical place we moved in together, alone. I remember that I felt safe then, and cherished. I remember that I loved him.

That's the thing about memory; it swirls around your life and makes a pretty picture to play such scenes against. All I really had of my father then was his presence. It's easy now to see why I was compelled by the landscape under our small boat: I had become accustomed to peeking in at other worlds; I believed something wonderful would take my hook. I always hoped to catch the big one.

All the fishermen from both sides of the *Indian Days,* midships back, rush to help my father when he falls. The stern begins to lower and the skipper tells people to move forward, they're unbalancing the boat. They help him up, wipe off all the fish blood. The skipper stands back a bit, says a few words about his not being responsible for "personal" safety. My father doesn't say anything at all. He works his thin lips vigorously and spittle gathers in the corners of his mouth. Although no one voices it, the greatest concern is that we might have to turn back because my father has been injured. This is the event of the summer for some of them, a week's wage to spend a whole day out at sea. They don't want it to be ruined by some old guy who shouldn't have been there in the first place.

He does have a lump on the back of his head, but otherwise, he's just shaken up. Trudy turns out to be a nurse, and she looks at his pupils, runs reassuring hands over his neck and back.

"Hey, Harry," she grins at him, giving him a big hug. "You didn't have to *fall* for me. I'm pretty easy!" Over his shoulder she gives me a thumbs up and a sweet encouraging smile. "Just had the wind knocked out," she mouths. What has really been knocked out of him is hope. He knows now as I knew earlier that he will not be catching any good fish, not now, not ever.

The *Indian Days'* engine turns over as the skipper heads to a different spot. Shake off the bad luck. The fishermen go back to their places on the rail. My father hardly notices he has lost one of his best rods, so great is his fear. He can't bear to be above deck and makes his way painfully below, where rough wooden benches line either side. I ease him down on one and sit beside him. I try to convince him he should try up top again. Dad's not talking. He's not even looking at me. He's sitting slumped on the bench in the dark interior of the boat, her bare ribs cradling him on either side, slow tears running down his face.

The afternoon passes in shrouded silence. Every so often someone comes below to get a beer out of his cooler, use the head. Trudy checks in. My father is dozing, lolled back against the rough wood. He looks like a vagrant, his clothes dirty and bloodied, his pant leg torn. I pass the time in a suspended state, afraid to leave him and go on deck, even though I would love to fish; reluctant to read or write. This is like a bedside vigil. It's not polite to scribble away when you're minding the sick. I try to think nurturing thoughts about my father, try to send healing signals into his scrambled brain. Like Claudius at prayer, I am a sham: "My words fly up, my thoughts remain below." The truth is, I have no healing signals for my father. The truth is, he has been so little involved in my life, I can hardly think of him as my father.

The summer I left Cedar, I took to roaming the town at night. Most evenings there were only kids running around, but Thursday was the night the farmers came to trade their wares and stock up. The lone four stores stayed open late, and the tavern hummed. My grandfather operated a creamery at the bottom of Main Street. On one such Thursday night a few weeks before they put me on the southbound bus, I looked downhill in the crepuscular light to where the steam rolled out of his creamery—sulfurous, hissing, luminous as an epiphany: a glimpse into a nether world where offerings glowed before a primitive altar and dark shapes moved between the shadows and the firelight. I imagined my grandfather there, small, sinewy, sweat-drenched in dark wool trousers and a white undershirt vest with suspenders, moving in and out of the yellow vapor, lifting the heavy silver milk cans out of the gaping boilers and placing them on the old scale while farmers leaned in his doorway, faceless, smoking and passing a pint bottle, listening to the Detroit Tigers on his old square Zenith.

It seemed that already my childhood had passed into mythology, that my distance from my grandparents, from the life I had known for the past nine years, was lengthening.

The engine fires and the *Indian Days* swings around and starts back in.

The vibration rouses my father. He looks around him suspiciously, his gaze finally falling on me.

"You didn't take good care of me," he says matter-of-factly. I don't deny it. He puts his hands on his knees and starts to get up.

"I have to go to the bathroom," he says. Midships there is a cubicle head, a small unisex stall with a wooden door.

"It's right there," I gesture. He looks straight at me. "I have to go to the bathroom," he says. I get it. He needs help to negotiate the swaying motion of the boat as she plows ahead toward Portland Harbor. I get up and put my hand under his arm, help him up, help him across the ten feet to the stall door. I prop it open and help him over the rough, raised threshold. The convenience is an open commode with no lid. The stench is strong from a season of beer drinkers. Dad shuffles the two feet into the cubicle and stands before the hole. I'm outside, closing the door. He looks over his shoulder.

"You have to help me," he says. For a fleeting minute, I think he's kidding. For another, I wonder just what "help" means. The cubicle is really too small for both of us, but I squeeze in, step behind him and around on the far side so I'm between the commode and the wall, almost facing him. The cramped space forces me to crouch down. He's leaning with both hands on the two walls to steady himself.

He looks at me and then nods below. Below. I reach across and unzip his pants. My hands are shaking and I'm afraid I'm going to hurt him. He's still looking at the wall, waiting. There must be more. I take a deep breath and reach inside his pants, inside the flap of his underwear and withdraw his penis. My vision blurs. I pull his penis out and aim it at the bowl, trying to touch him with just the tips of two fingers. He begins to pee, a sharp thin arc.

In that instant, in the flash of the urine, its scent, I realize I have seen this before: when I was a child and we were fishing up the Cedar River, I remember now that he urinated off the bow of the boat, a stronger sharp arc. I remember that I, an only child with no brothers, no male cousins, had never seen a penis before. I remember thinking how thick and powerful it looked. How it reminded me of the fat water hyacinth root. My fingers stiffen. The penis I'm holding now is withered and gray, the testicles shrunken back into his groin; the springing copper bush I remember from before, white and wispy. The flow falls off.

He looks at me then, meeting my tear-filled eyes. "Shake it," he says, what could be a smile playing on his tight pink lips. The *Indian Days* turns into a wave and I lose my balance, sliding down the narrow wall.

I am looking up at him.

The afternoon brightens perceptively as the *Indian Days* nears port. This is a familiar Maine phenomenon. Because the North Atlantic is so cold, when the air is warm, as in summer, there is almost always fog out to sea, condensed from the antipodal temperatures colliding. When there is an offshore breeze, it is sunny along the coast; when there is an onshore breeze, the fog penetrates to perhaps a half mile before being turned back by the big pines, seized upon and dissipated by warmer earth vapors. Today, there is an offshore breeze, so we can see the sun glowing ahead of us like the dawn as we near land, a virtual goal we seem to steer for. There is always a moment on days like these when the ship actually breaks out of the fog and is suddenly blinded by sunshine, blue skies, soft, impossible clouds. It's like turning a lens from soft focus to hard, a sharpness of detail that hurts the eyes. When it happens today, it is especially jarring, making everything that happened out at sea, out under the cover of fog, seem to be even more distant and unreal.

My father remains below, sitting on a bench near the aft hatchway. I have taken a place above, at the stern rail, watching the sea, the fog, fall away behind us as we steam into Portland Harbor. When I turn back, I can see him at the bottom of the passageway talking to a couple of fishermen who are below now, gathering up their gear. He looks animated. He's holding up his left hand, palm flexed and away from him, pointing to the area below his thumb. I know he's showing them where he lives in Michigan. Ask anyone from Michigan where he lives and he immediately flips up his hand, demonstrating the mitten. I even do it myself sometimes. It's funny, isn't it, to be able to show anyone from anywhere in this country your exact location on the map? It makes it seem like you know where you are.

Nat Leach Brook

I came to think of water in a different way during the years I lived with Peter in Limington, a rural township at the edge of Maine's Western Mountains near the New Hampshire border. I had not been inland in years. Salt air always filled my senses. I had not considered the relationship between the water and the land. An ocean person, I lived on the rim of the coast where water delineated, washed ashore from distant lands and left its detritus, but did not interact. A sailor, I was at home with tides and currents. Fresh water was not in my ken. Yet I was drawn to it in Limington, listening for its presence in the woodland; sitting for hours beside vernal pools high up on the ridges, watching the miniature flora there, frogbit, looking for planktonic floating organisms. I followed Nat Leach Brook into the woods.

Nat Leach enters Peter's tree farm through a culvert under the Boothby Road, a quarter of a mile east of his house, just above the old orchard by the logging trail. The goshawk on high sees the brooklet strike straight out from the Little Ossipee River, dash across the meadows and encroaching alders, fall momentarily just before the road into a gulping pool above the culvert where in spring boys both young and old cast their lines for trout, and slide under the road—safe!—having gained the tangle of the tree farm on the other side. No meanderer, our Nat.

It sneaks in like a little wet spot that spreads, a leak that cannot be found: swampy, mossy, rising to shine around rough-edged rocks now ground to smooth, round river stone over centuries of freshet. Once across the road, it pauses, and spreads out, satisfied, claiming as much ground as it can cover; uncertain of its next move. Nat Leach keeps the swamp maples' feet wet all year round, stunting their growth but giving them the tradeoff of the earliest red leaves of autumn, often in August. The brook falls down some more boulders into a much bigger marsh, then hits the ridge climbing beyond where the house stands to end its run below the old spruce plantation. Not a bad end from that first impulse away from the mother Ossipee. Nearly two miles in all, enough to gain a name, not anonymous like some other escapees from the river who, unidentified, form miles of soggy surrounds just above where the Little Ossipee rejoins the mighty Saco.

An old story. Rivers, like children and countries, often cannot decide what they want to be, how much power or control they want to embrace and channel, and so, let nature take its course. They are shaped by events and the vagaries of forces outside themselves: become lawyers when they really wanted to be poets; enact trade agreements when they thought they were committed to letting the market rule. Rivers become damned up, self-important, when just a splash would have done. They go off in directions it will take years of therapy or legislation to reverse. Consider the Platt, cutting through all that sandstone, trying a little of this, a little of that, silting up first one bank and then another. Growing cities in the desert. Settling the west in a different direction. Or the Whitewater, pristine, nurturing fat bass until it was damned up to flood over unfortunate backwoods whose only sin was being there, transmogrified into a household word that defined a generation of politicos trolling for the truth.

The history of Maine is a history of rivers, of concourse and congress, of people being transported to places where they did not belong on the back of running water. Maine is a state shaped by water—fresh, salted, frozen: water that gushed unchecked down the sides of mountains; water dragged high up the rocky shores by a moon tipping off the edge of the continent; water frozen into ice blades gouging out lakes like Oedipus's eyes. Runaway tides on the shore. Ice fields slipping off a Canadian high up north, crunching pine trees before them like the toothpicks that would one day be fashioned out of the broiling churning logs woodsmen rode downstream to Limington, a town which took its name from the sheared appendages of trees.

When Peter came to Limington in the 1970s, he altered the course of Nat Leach Brook. Before he came, before he bought the land that was among the original dozen parcels mapped out in those rich curling hands of Limington's founding settlers in the 1770s, whose penmanship indicates some higher purpose than the lumbering avarice they apparently served, for all those years before Peter, Nat Leach Brook was undisciplined, seldom contained except in drought: a primordial wetland.

Peter was a man of action in those days. Where an owner before him had halfheartedly damned up Nat Leach to form a kind of muddy fishing hole near the cabin where he would later build the house, Peter employed backhoes and engineering to create more than two acres of serious water. Where the brook flowed naturally downhill toward some bigger rocks, gathering strength and definition, Peter built a high square dam, a box of concrete fully twenty feet long, ten feet wide, and ten feet deep, dropping, like locks, every two feet, down to an open spreading maw, giant stone and cement wings flying out from a perfectly poured mouth.

This sort of thing is done in summer, when water flows the least, when it is easy to divert and fool it. That first summer I spent in Limington, I found a packet of old photographs in a box way in the back of a closet shelf documenting the harnessing of Nat Leach Brook. Younger, vigorous, Peter stands in the middle of the dry dam, his arms reaching out to either side and not quite touching. The walls loom above his head, and he is over six feet tall. He's grinning, legs spread wide in khaki shorts with lots of working pockets. The next shot is pulled back, taken from the road on the far side of the dam, near where the house will stand. It shows a wide expanse of sculpted clay, the dry pond's bones, smoothed out and sloping to twenty feet deep in the center, rounded but oblong, ovate, with the dam at one point, Nat Leach Brook regaining itself at the other to flow under a quaint rounded bridge and on into the forest. In the center sits the backhoe, yellow and muscular. Peter leans on its bucket, triumphant, smiling widely at whoever took these pictures.

The pond Peter built—which, unlike Nat Leach Brook, did not have a name—found its way on to geological surveys. It appears shining and distinct on both the State of Maine Topographical Map No. 111 (Limington Village) and on aviation charts of the area, a landmark reflecting back God's eye, possessed now of cardinal points, projection, scale. Pilots honing in on the Limington airfield, a grassy strip some five miles from the tree farm, take a bearing on the pond for an approach from the east, the most common in a land of prevailing westerlies. Their flyover was a daily occurrence, and often they would dip their wings in friendly salute as they passed over me hanging clothes out to dry. Their salutes made me feel official.

I was there. The place where Peter and I began to live out our life was marked on a chart, all measured out, plumbed by a legend. Such validation does not come easily. It reassured me that I had been accounted for. Located.

The pond created from Nat Leach Brook was, by the time I came to Limington, the reference point for all forays into the tree farm: you went to the pond and turned either left or right; went uphill or back beyond. Inside the house, you felt as though you were on a ship at sea. Because its entire south side facing the pond was glass, and because the pond sat only thirty feet away, all you could see from inside the house was water. Sunlight reflecting off it chased across the ceilings. The wind crossing and recrossing the pond, created sheets of texture, different light. Endlessly, it drew the eye. Tirelessly, it pleased. At dusk, in the fading light above the dam, herons flew silhouetted against a velvet sky. Over the towering black fir, the lights of planes lowering into the Portland Jetport thirty miles away lent just enough track and symmetry to keep us grounded.

The wash of water in Peter's pond was a constant keeping our life on course, a rhythm that calmed us. Perhaps for longer than we might otherwise have been. Or I might otherwise have been. The overriding fact of life in Limington was that it was, and had been for many years, Peter's. He let me in. He did not accommodate me. I was what he needed to complete his scene. Seeing it all through new eyes, I did not realize that the canvas had long been dry. I thought I had a brush myself, figured I could choose a color. I didn't understand that by becoming part of the landscape, I had taken myself out of the picture.

By following Nat Leach up into the tree farm, I learned to recognize the damselfly, even her nymph just under the clear surface, surrounded by necklaces of toad spawn. Intrigued by the workings of the gravity-fed well, I peered down daily into its glaucous depths, gauging the ebb and flow, measuring our supply. I learned what all those settlers before me must have learned, that so many things in Limington worked by natural force, followed a course long ago established, independent of outside interests. In the beginning, I did not apply that lesson to myself. In the beginning, like Twain's innocent river pilot, "I had made a valuable acquisition." In the end, when I had mastered the language of Peter's woods, like Twain, " ... I had lost something, too. I had lost something which could never be restored to me while I lived. All the grace, the beauty, the poetry had gone...."

I rinsed the crusted salt off my kayak and put it in the Saco. The Saco River, named after an Indian chief or tribe like all of the great rivers of Maine—the Penobscot, the Kennebec, the Androscoggin—rises out of its headwaters at Saco Lake, high in the White Mountains of northern New Hampshire. The Saco drops nearly fifteen hundred feet in elevation in the one hundred twenty miles it runs before emptying into the Atlantic Ocean at Ferry Beach in a town and bay that bear its name. Where it flows through Limington, the Saco drops fifty feet at the "Rips," a series of rapids just above the elbow of the Little Ossipee.

I crossed the Rips nearly every day when I lived in Limington, on my way to shop or to run errands. I never failed to marvel at the tumble and tumult of the river there. In autumn I walked the banks of the Little Ossipee nearly up to the Saco, transversing fields just below the tree farm. What once was primeval pine forest, trees whose trunks made the masts of schooners, had been replaced by scrub growth, stunted stock. Change was not so apparent in the river. It appeared the same, and invited me to imagine what it might have been like there when Limington was settled. Even now, there was little development along the corridor. Even now, I could walk up to the edge of this great river, my footsteps muffled by hundreds of years of pine needles, and watch the water surge past me, strong and wide and deep. I expected to see a dugout of Sawatucket coming around the bend upstream.

I lived in my head when I lived in Limington. My vision was cast back. Separated by choice as well as culture and space from my friends and family, I was suspended in a world I made up out of my own dreamy needs and the history I hungrily absorbed about the place. I thought about Cornelia "Flyrod" Crosby, as I thought about many figures from the town's past. They all seemed more real to me than its present-day inhabitants. I felt at one with the past, alienated from my neighbors.

Cornelia Crosby came from Phillips, Maine, a logging community near Mount Blue in those same Western Mountains feeding our own spring freshets. She might have stood on the banks of the Saco herself, watching water very much the same surge by. Carefully and highly educated in the academies of the 1800s, six-foot-tall Cornelia developed a nervous condition at her first job as a bookkeeper in Strong, Maine, possibly the effect of tuberculosis. Her doctor advised her to take the mountain air, and so Cornelia, in her early twenties, walked what would become the Appalachian Trial, and cajoled local fishermen to teach her how to cast. She took to the woods faster than Louise Dickinson Rich, and became a poster girl for "Vacationland," a word she coined for Maine in 1895 at the first Sportsman's Show in

Madison Square Garden where she lugged an honest-to-goodness log cabin, some balsam fir, and a whole steel tank full of brown trout she cast into and caught. Cornelia wrote a fishing column she signed "Flyrod Crosby," to conceal her sex, and went on to become Maine's first licensed guide (male or female) before succumbing to Catholicism and ending her days among the Sisters of Mercy, back in those same Western Mountains. She used the last of her funds to build a rustic chapel in Quossoc, just up the road from Peter in Rangeley.

Pictures of Flyrod in her prime show a strikingly handsome woman, tall and slim with strong features, wearing a split leather skirt and fringed hat. Legend has it that when she went into the woods to fish she carried her creel and a basket of pink linens and fine china for tea beside a stream. I liked to imagine her striding out of a thicket ahead of me, elaborate bamboo rod in hand; or nestled, ladylike, on the moss by the side of Nat Leach Brook. She never married but drank her whiskey straight with Theodore Roosevelt on the shore of Moosehead Lake where she tutored him in catching salmon. A picture shows the two of them in a graceful bark canoe, Teddy paddling and Flyrod sitting demurely in the bow, trailing one hand in the water for all the world like a nymph on the Thames. A fine string of shining fish decorates the center thwart.

She became my alter ego when I first moved to Limington. When I followed Nat Leach Brook into the woods in an attempt to delineate my life there, I was talking all the time in my head to Flyrod Crosby. Surely, I could make sense of this if she did. I romanticized my journey as I romanticized her journey.

I was thinking of her on an early autumn night after my first summer in Limington, wondering what had happened in her life to change her from the confident journalist of her youth to the diminished pious convert of her later years, when Peter beckoned me to come outside, under the overhanging pines, up to the side of a pool in Nat Leach Brook, above the pond and just behind the house. Here the water slowed and widened to eight feet, circled all around by mossy lips of reddish rock. The pool was only three feet deep; the bottom, soft sand and tiny, pearl-white pebbles. He was carrying a flashlight and shone it into the water near a stone shelf. Caught there in the circle of light, stunning against the bleached sand bottom, were two trout, gilded golden brown, blood-red speckled with brilliant azure side fins. The female, a little duller, swam under the shelf and spewed forth a cloud of eggs; the male, vibrant with color, swam around and over her, fanning his tail across the eggs, spewing forth a different nebulae. Together their tails swept and turned, each head at a different end, circling slowly in a water waltz unmistakably familiar.

    Peter took my hand. We knelt on the soft bank watching the trout mate. The air was heady with the decay of fall: the sour brown scent of wet leaves rotting, the red taste of pollen dusting, the tang of virid moss releasing spore. All suspended in the sharp tannic fragrance of spring water. I shivered. Peter put his arm around me, pulling me in. He smelled of tobacco and Irish whiskey, lavender and wool.

    "You see the life we'll have?" he said, the only words he spoke. Overhead the moon spun and the owl called, and something scooted through the bushes. The trout glided past, around and around.

    Of course I saw.

When Lilacs Last

I.

South Paris, Maine, the rural shire town of Oxford County, tumbles along the edge of the foothills of the Western Mountains. Its only claim to dubious fame is as the manufacturer (long defunct) of the "American Flyer," that sled of "Rosebud" renown. In the summer of 1996, a group of locals began picketing a big old house on Main Street, waving signs proclaiming "Save the Garden." The object of their concern was behind that house, a four-acre perennial garden created by Bernard McLaughlin, a man identified in northeastern horticultural circles as the "Dean of Maine Gardeners."

Tucked behind a white picket fence north of the house—which is situated on a busy street of fast-food restaurants and gas stations—the garden is entered by an arbored gate down at its far end. Truly secret and palpably charming, the McLaughlin Garden is an informal collection of beds and trees along wide grassy avenues in the English cottage garden style. Bernard, the son of potato farmers from Limestone, Maine, married into the Main Street property in 1936. Over the next sixty years of digging up and planting, of transplanting and "scratching" around a little fertilizer here and there, he fashioned an incredible collection of lilacs, irises, ferns, hosta, lady slippers, and *semper virens*, the common hens n' chickens. The space is testimony to his astonishing vigor, good health, and single-minded devotion. At the age of ninety he still worked ten hours a day in the garden at the steady and careful pace he had always maintained.

Gradually word spread, first among gardeners, and then—a feature article here, a television special there—among the populace. By the mid-1980s, five thousand visitors a summer were strolling through Bernard's garden gate, marveling at his ability to keep a continuous display of color and interest all through the season from the first splashy spring bulbs through the somber glowing chrysanthemums of autumn. On Sundays, he strolled around the garden with them, dressed in his pale blue suit from Mass. He was a handsome man with fine features, a high forehead, bright blue eyes, a full head of wavy white hair. Robust, decorous. Visitors to the garden during this period made numerous videotapes. These tapes have been donated to the McLaughlin Foundation and form the basis of an extensive video library documenting both Bernard McLaughlin and stages in the garden's evolution. Print accounts repeatedly quote people who ask to "meet the famous gardener," only to be told he is the quiet old gentleman down on his hands and knees behind the smoke bush just off the wide green path. The videos, however, reveal McLaughlin in his avuncular mode. Pointing out special wildflower blooms under the fronds of a gigantic fern or gesturing to a vista of blue sky behind the tricolor beech, he says, "Now isn't that a fantastic sight?"

Bernard McLaughlin famously stated "sharing this garden with others is my great satisfaction," a statement first published in *Downeast Magazine* in 1986 that is now engraved on a plaque in the garden, and features prominently on all of the McLaughlin Foundation's literature. He never charged admission. But when he died in 1995 at the age of ninety-eight, he made no provision for preservation of the garden in his will. That's when the brouhaha ensued. That's when it became clear that there were decidedly different notions about "saving the garden," and that those notions split clearly down the line separating the locals from the transplants, the people "from away."

I had a peripheral sense of this at the time. I remember seeing a newspaper article headlined "They're fighting over the flowers again," but it wasn't until I met my husband Ed Robinson in 1998 that the details were brought home to me. He had lived near South Paris in the late 1980s. A student of horticulture as well as a landscape contractor, Ed had introduced himself to Bernard and asked to be taken on as an apprentice one day a week in the garden. Thus it was that he came to know the old man, to work alongside him, to share the tasty simple lunches Bernard—formerly a chef—prepared for him, and for Bernard's son Richard, who was working for his father in those days, weeding, mowing, trimming around the edges.

The first time I saw the McLaughlin Garden was at the end of October in 1999, when Ed pulled in next to the arbored gate, glowing in late afternoon autumn sunshine. We were on our way to somewhere else, and, on impulse, he "had" to show me Bernard's garden. We entered the silent space as shadows lengthened and a last thermal breath of breeze lifted the leaves around us. The dusty heads of a few mums already nipped by frost stood up against the mostly brown landscape. Ferns waved bright saffron on the hillside. We walked the paths brittle with dead grass, and Ed pointed out plants that had bloomed here, would bloom there. The lilacs stood sentinel overhead, leafless, their slender, budded branches reaching into the lowering sky. It was a tour of the imagination.

Dusk was settling in, that autumnal crepuscular light that both glows gold and gathers darkness from the shadows. We were on the backside of the hosta bed, walking down the hill from the site of the wildflower garden when a large shape startled and leaped away from us, crashing noisily through the yellow ferns. I jumped, even knowing—as I saw the white flag flash—that it was a deer.

It would be another two years before I came to realize there were many forces at work in the McLaughlin Garden to make me jump, and that some of them, like the deer I saw on my first visit, moved silently through fading light, feral, alien to the careful cultivation around them: fully intent on purposes known only to the rank and wild.

II.

Ed's stories of Bernard McLaughlin, of his garden, and of the difficulties surrounding its acquisition by the folks from away percolated through me for a couple of years before I decided to go up to South Paris and speak to Lee Dassler, Executive Director of the McLaughlin Foundation. I called to make an appointment, briefly outlining my interest in writing about the garden. She knew Ed because he had continued a peripheral involvement with the site, occasionally volunteering both advice and labor. Since Maine is a small state, the horticulture people know each other. She offered to meet with me the following week.

When I met with Lee Dassler for the first time in January 2002, I couldn't imagine someone wasn't already writing a book about Bernard McLaughlin. There had been hundreds of articles and the subject appeared to me to be a perfect project. I was surprised, therefore, at Lee's enthusiastic response to my suggestion at our first meeting. They would be delighted. I was new to this kind of writing. My experience was journalistic, but always under the aegis of a sponsoring organization. I had never struck out on my own in this way before. Suddenly, here I was, anointed by the McLaughlin Foundation. I was offered a desk in the archives, which were made completely available to me.

What does a writer do in an archive? I had never worked in one before. I spent whole days in the office—on the second floor of Bernard's house on Main Street—leafing through old deeds and photographs of dead people who had lived in northern Maine. I read pages and pages of reports of the harvest on the land that eventually became the garden behind the old Tribou homestead. How many bushels of wheat and apples. I wrote it all down. I looked at Bernard's marriage certificate and discharge from the U.S. Army. I read the original handwritten copy of his valedictory address from Limestone High School in 1918, tied with a purple ribbon. I looked out the window at the garden.

After one such early session, I wandered down to Bernard's kitchen, which has become quite upscale and high tech, a twenty-foot-square room of stainless steel sinks and granite countertops, a big Garland range. Even though Bernard had been a chef, I don't think he ever had a kitchen like this one. Lee was making perfect little scones for volunteers from Paris Hill who were helping Kristin Perry, the new horticulturalist from New York, to repot seedlings for the upcoming spring plant sale. It was late March, and the garden was still mostly under snow. I stood beside Lee at the sink, looking out the window across the wrecked space, all twisted stalks and smashed branches.

"I can't help but look up on the ridge to see if he's there," Lee said, rinsing off a baking tin.

"Who?" I asked.

"Richard," she said.

"Do you mean Richard McLaughlin?" I asked, for her answer surprised me.

"Of course I mean Richard McLaughlin," Lee said, turning toward me. "He's out there early most mornings, up on the ridge. He walks around the edge of the garden. He's looking for something." She dried her hands and leaned her back against the counter. "Whatever you do in your piece," she said earnestly, "you must not bring up Richard."

Now I was more than surprised. Richard was the story. Even that early in the process, I was struck by the biblical implications of this tale, the authoritative father, the wayward son, expulsion from the garden. But I was new to my role there. Lytton Strachey once said, "… it is perhaps as difficult to write a good life as to live one." My position was steeped in naiveté. And claustrophobia. I didn't realize that I was entirely too close to my sources and lacked aesthetic distance. Soon I would begin to see how everyone connected with the McLaughlin Garden had some stake in my perspective.

"We can't go through this again," Lee said. "It's too dangerous for everyone involved. I don't think I could bear it." I did not reply.

Only a few days later, I was included in a relatively big event, the delivery by Bernard's nephew John Kelleher of boxes of McLaughlin family memorabilia. Lee had initially asked me to sit in on the Saturday when John brought this treasure to the Foundation, but as it turned out, she was occupied with participants in one of their programs, "Choosing Spring Shrubs." John and I spent the morning alone together in her office, talking and going through the documents. I was struck by two things: the loving care with which John Kelleher unburdened himself of decades of lore and anecdote; and the affection with which he spoke of his cousin Richard Tribou

McLaughlin. John Kelleher was the first person to make me really want to talk to Richard.

"Lee says he lurks around the garden," I told John. He is a contained man in his early fifties with a bluff Irish demeanor and an accompanying lack of self-esteem. Of average size and height, he was neatly dressed in an L.L. Bean uniform: cords, plaid shirt, good unused hiking boots.

"Oh, well," John said. "I haven't seen Richard in a while, but, you know, *lurks* is not a word for Richard. He's not easy with people like Lee and the others here at the Foundation." He was shuffling through his pictures and letters. His hands are soft, well taken care of. "This is his home," he said. "It's his home."

III.

Serendipity brought Lee Dassler together with the from-away contingent who were involved in saving Bernard's garden in 1996. Because of her background in historical preservation (she was at that time employed restoring an old homestead in nearby Bolster Mills, Maine), someone who knew someone called Lee about how to negotiate the National Registry to begin the process of listing a property on the National Register. The project caught her interest, and she became the center around which the from-away pole swung. She also became the polarizing factor in the save-the-garden movement, the dynamic dividing the preservationists.

Initially during that summer of 1996—six months after Bernard's death and when the sign out front announcing that the Main Street property was for sale alerted the public—the save-the-garden people were a mixed lot. A number of them, led by Walter Bressette, a close friend of Bernard's adopted son Richard McLaughlin, were local people, and their overriding concern was to keep the garden as it had been when Bernard was there. The from-away faction—led soon by Lee Dassler—saw the survival of the garden in terms of grants and federal protective actions, such as the National Registry.

There was never any suggestion that Richard—or any heir—questioned Bernard's decision to convert all of his assets, including the garden, to currency to satisfy his bequests. Richard never "lost" the garden—a perception floating around the edges of the conflict at the time. Rather, Richard couldn't afford to buy the garden (which really meant buying the property, buying the house). He also never indicated that he wanted to. Six months before Bernard's death, on June 5, 1995, an article appeared in the Lewiston *Sun Journal* stating that Bernard and Richard Tribou McLaughlin were preparing a fifteen-acre site in Greenwood, Maine (a few miles away, where Richard owned property) for the transplantation of all of Bernard's stock. Both Bernard and Richard are quoted in the article discussing this plan. Since his father had promised before his death that the plants belonged to Richard to do with what he would, Richard seemed happy simply to transplant. It's likely it didn't occur to Richard to even attempt to buy the property until he saw the situation in its larger context. A group of people could buy the garden and run it as an "arboretum" (Richard and his friend Walter Bressette always used that word to describe the garden's "preserved" configuration), that he and his sons could "caretake." At the time of Bernard's death, Richard had been "caretaking" (his word) the garden for over a decade, since his return from the Indian pilgrimage in the early 1980s that made him a Buddhist. For the last year or so of Bernard's life, Richard and his son Tony (who was in his early twenties at the time) were caretaking the property together. They continued to do so on into the summer of 1996 when the hubbub ensued. Once this arboretum/caretaking notion took hold, Richard and his friends joined the save-the-garden action enthusiastically.

It is worth noting that Richard's group identified itself as the Bernard McLaughlin Preservation Committee. The preservation notion is strong in upcountry Maine, as it is in many rural areas. It means keeping the *status quo*, a variation on "if it ain't broke, don't fix it." The fundamental difference between the local group and the one from away was between "preservation" and "conservation," a subtle (and in this case, defining) distinction. Although Lee Dassler talked about "preserving" historic property, what she really meant was to keep it intact and allow it to evolve organically. She saw the "landscape" of Bernard's garden as being the context in which his plants prospered. She was strongly opposed to transplanting the garden. In an interview with Paul Tukey published in *People, Places and Plants* in the spring of 1998, just a year after her group had secured the garden she said:

> Perhaps, in some cases, it would make more sense to save the collection of plants that could be transplanted entirely to another location or split up. The town would lose the gardener, but not the garden, in effect. But this garden is different. Bernard's garden seems to me to be a design; this was a landscape. And to take the plants out of this landscape and spread them out would have destroyed something here. On top of this, I think of this as having been a public park for 60 years since Bernard allowed people to come as they wanted to. ... I think there is something also to be said for our design landscapes and our cultural landscapes, that the history should be preserved and not forgotten. How we rally

the resources to do that may require a reassessment of our values.

The Bernard McLaughlin Preservation Committee was just that: preservation of Bernard McLaughlin. They did not want any outsiders involved in the garden. They did not want there to be anything different from the way it had been when Bernard was there. Today it seems obvious that this was a short-sighted approach. Bernard was not there. He had not, in some sense, been there for the last few years before his death as his health and vigor declined. While the local group never articulated it, it also seems possible that they saw the garden not as an opportunity to give back to the community a treasure but rather as a means to ensure personal livelihood (caretaking) and perhaps even gain (admission). To *conserve* is to keep from loss, decay, waste, or injury. To *preserve* is to keep alive or in existence. That slight tilt toward stasis rendered the locals dormant.

Everyone was raising money—locals, transplants, even businesses—which was arriving willy-nilly at the South Paris post office, often addressed simply "McLaughlin Garden." It was Lee Dassler's authoritative posture that forced the group to splinter. She could and would speak only from her perspective as a preserver of historical places. She could and did see only one way to approach this situation. Since no one else knew any way at all, it was literally her way or the highway. The McLaughlin Preservation Committee made a couple of half-hearted attempts to rally, but they were done in by their Maine diffidence. To a bunch of country boys, the ladies from up on Paris Hill (an exclusive, restored historical village within the township that showcases the estate of Hannibal Hamlin, Lincoln's vice-president and a governor of Maine) and Lee Dassler appeared formidable.

The two groups couldn't agree on how the money should be spent, so a judge just down the street at the Oxford County Courthouse froze the funds at the post office. By the time an arbitrator was brought up from Boston in August 1996 to decide who should get the contributions, there wasn't even anyone present from the local group to state their case.

And it was Lee who demonized Richard McLaughlin. During the summer of the save-the-garden conflict, Richard was informally authorized to transplant stock from the garden. His father had told him he could (as reported in the 1995 *Sun Journal* article), and John Jenness, the estate's attorney, had assured Richard the verbal promise was binding. All that summer, he and his son Tony were around the property. As it became clear that the Bernard McLaughlin Preservation Committee was not going to prevail in its effort to save the garden from the forces from away, Richard's transplanting efforts intensified. Initially, Lee Dassler—following attorney Jenness's advice—agreed that Richard could continue to transplant the stock, and she and Richard reached an agreement whereby he would leave at least one of each specimen in place. *Sun Journal* reporter Judith Meyers, who was talking to both Richard and Dassler during this period, reported that Richard was satisfied with this compromise, and hoped to be able to parlay it into a situation where he and his sons could continue to caretake the garden.

But something happened—Meyers says that Lee just did not want Richard around—and only a week later, the Foundation moved to obtain an injunction against Richard's removing any additional stock. At around the same time, Lee called the sheriff when Richard came onto the property, and the *Sun Journal* carried the headline on

August 16, 1996, "Lawyer hired in effort to halt moving of flowers." Very soon thereafter, "someone" entered the garden by night, removed large numbers of plants (in some instances, all the stock), and cut the identifying tags off all those remaining. From then on, Richard was described as "lurking."

Lee told me how Richard had followed her nights down the winding rural roads out from South Paris to her home in Bolster Mills. She said she was "terrified." She told me that Richard invited her to see where he had planted Bernard's extraordinary and rare blue hosta stock, and that she had walked with him deep into the woods outside of town one afternoon. She said he had carried a machete, and she had been "terrified." She told me that Richard had heeled in the plants in the woods, and that they had all died. She said he'd taken Bernard's horticulture card files out of the house and burned them.

When I repeated those details to Judith Meyers, who wrote more than thirty articles about the McLaughlin garden and about the acquisition conflict, she scoffed, "Oh that's ridiculous."

Judy is an attractive, no-nonsense woman who was Oxford County Bureau Chief for nearly twenty years for the paper recently judged to be the best in Maine.

"Lee Dassler isn't 'terrified.' This is the woman who called the police when Richard McLaughlin stepped near the property during the summer of 1996, when ostensibly he was authorized to be transplanting the garden. I cannot believe that anyone followed Lee Dassler down a dark road and she didn't call the cops. Or that she doesn't call the cops any time she thinks he's around the garden now. Lee Dassler likes the drama." Judy went on to tell me that one night during that eventful summer when she needed to check facts with Lee about an article she was writing for the paper, Lee was only able to speak with her after eight on a Saturday night.

"I was going to the Oxford Plains Speedway with my family," Judy said, referring to the race track that is the biggest draw in the county, "so I called her from a pay phone outside the stadium. She gave me all this grief about how a woman of 'your standing in the community' should know better than to be frequenting such a lowlife place as the speedway." Judith Meyers grew up on Long Island. There does not appear to be anything *lowlife* about her. She's earnest and serious, eminently respectable. In 2003, Judith Meyers was named "Maine Journalist of the Year" by the Maine Press Association.

"There are certain kinds of people who are not acceptable to Lee Dassler," Judy said. "Richard is one of them." Richard did not destroy the records, she told me. "They mean too much to him," she said. "They mean everything to him."

IV.

Walter Bressette, the local man who had been prominent in the initial save-the-garden conflict, put me in touch with Richard Tribou McLaughlin. Bressette responded by e-mail to my "Author Seeks Assistance" ad in the Norway, Maine, *Advertiser Democrat* in March, 2002. His tone was both condescending and defensive. Essentially, he said, whatever it is you want to know, we can tell you, and it will be "the *real story*." He identified himself as the Bernard McLaughlin Preservation Committee, but I recognized his name from the sender tag line as a person who had been dragged, literally, out of a McLaughlin Foundation board meeting in the summer of 1996 by the Oxford County Sheriff, the man whose picture was on the front page of the *Advertiser Democrat* under the headline "They're fighting over the flowers again."

When I first heard from Bressette, I forwarded the e-mail to Lee Dassler, asking her "who are these folks?" Her response was quite emotional. She identified them as part of the "anti-faction," and Walter in particular as a friend of Richard's. She asked me "on behalf of the protection of the garden" not to respond to him. "My job," she said, "is to protect and preserve this resource—and there is still a palatable [sic] threat fifteen minutes away that I need to remain alert to." I was taken aback. I thought about it for a full day before I wrote back to her that the work would have no integrity if I did not at least consider all sources. I assured her that I was not trying to stir up trouble and would not encourage it, but that I had to hear whatever was out there. Lee is smart. Her response was gracious and complimentary as she stepped back from her original request "that you not respond to Walter," but a line had been crossed. From that point forward, Lee Dassler was less open to me and more guarded in her responses to my questions.

I wrote back to Walter Bressette saying I understood Richard McLaughlin was part of his group, and that I was interested in talking to Richard. Every time I corresponded with Walter, there was a day's hiatus before he responded. Obviously, he was conferring with his non-cyber buddy. Ultimately, Walter said I should get in touch with Richard myself directly. He gave me the unlisted number.

I called Richard a couple of times and got no answer, not even a machine. After a week, I e-mailed Walter that I hadn't been able to raise Richard and asked him to arrange a meeting at Shanters' coffee shop on Main Street in South Paris. I wasn't comfortable meeting Richard one-on-one. Ed had cautioned me about seeing Richard alone, and wanted to come with me. I knew Lee was physically afraid of Richard. Ed said Richard had an outlaw mentality and could go off unpredictably on political, survivalist rants. I didn't want Ed along, though. I wanted to meet Richard on my own terms, yet in a safe place. I thought the restaurant would work well.

I had no reply from Walter Bressette and tried Richard again. On an April Sunday, the day before I was going up to South Paris, I called him around noon. The phone rang and rang and rang before it was answered by a holler, "Barn!"

"May I speak to Richard McLaughlin, please?"

"You got 'em." When I started to identify myself, Richard interrupted me with a laugh. "Now how'd I know that was you?" He has a softened, enlightened, Maine accent, heightened country in places, backlit by mirth.

"Maybe because you have caller ID," I answered.

He laughed again. "No. I've been expecting you." I proposed meeting him at Shanters but Richard immediately said, "No I want you to come up here. I want you to see my gardens." He lives in Greenwood, about half an hour beyond South Paris. This wasn't shaping up the way I had planned. I demurred, saying I had interviews in town, and didn't have enough time to go back and forth.

"Well, suit yourself," Richard responded.

And then, in one of those moments of spontaneous, unconscious, capitulation, I said, "My husband Ed is going up to work on his Andover land tomorrow while I'm in South Paris. Maybe we can stop by either coming or going." So that's how it turned out that my first meeting with Richard Tribou McLaughlin was neither one-on-one, nor on my own terms. It was also nothing like I had expected.

That April Monday was Patriot's Day, a holiday only in Maine and Massachusetts, commemorating Paul Revere's Ride. There's no school, and it's the day they run the Boston Marathon. In western Maine, it had been raining all weekend, a steady hard slate rain, and Monday dawned raw, overcast and windy, the ragged clouds racing away, a little mist with fleeing showers in the air.

Spring comes different ways to Maine. In the city, spring is the increase of light and peeking early bulbs. In the country, spring is the melt and gush of ice-out, of winter rolling down the hills to the sea. On the way from Portland to South Paris, an hour-and-a-half drive, we cross the Crooked River at Bolster Mills and stop to marvel at the tumultuous water careering from side to side, bursting out from under the bridge, roaring through a grove of willows on the opposite bank.

By noon, when we head from South Paris out to Greenwood, some blue is showing in the sky. Here in the country it seems like a typical Maine April day: bare trees, some shadblow lighting up the edges of streams thundering down from the Oxford Hills. The sound of running water is everywhere.

Ed tells me the way to see Richard is just to drive around his rural neighborhood and we'll "run" into him. "That's the country way," Ed says. This has all gotten so beyond my control, I'm beginning to feel I'm just along for the ride. As we turn on to Route 219, along Mud Pond, a deceptively named sparkling body of water a couple of miles long fringed all around by foothills lined with white birch, Ed is telling me Richard stories. The chow he keeps in his dooryard to warn strangers away. How all the locals are afraid of him because he has something on their kids to whom he has sold drugs. We pass a cottage actually hanging over the water, just feet off the roadway. Two men are talking beside two pickups parked next to this structure.

Ed says, "Where'd you hear it first? There he is. That's Richard." We stop on the other side of the road, back up, get out and walk over.

The air is alive with sunlight glinting off the water. I feel like I'm walking through a shimmering fictive veil into another world. I'm glad we're in Ed's truck, not my Volvo. I'm glad I'm not alone.

Richard recognizes Ed and greets him warmly, even though they haven't met for several years. I shake hands and identify myself. He laughs and ducks his head in a self-deprecating gesture I will see him use a lot, almost a bow. "The new wife!" he says. "Good you got rid of the other one. She was a piece of work." The young man with him is probably one of his sons—he looks familiar to me, possibly from the newspaper archives at the foundation—a rugged, nice-looking young man in his mid-twenties. Richard does not introduce him, and the young man keeps his distance, making no move toward us. He does not seem surprised that Richard greets a couple of strangers enthusiastically who have stopped by the side of the road.

Richard explains that he caretakes this property, one of many on the pond that he claims he has "all sewn up." He says he caretakes a lot of property on the pond, and then owns the rest. His house, in fact, which Ed has pointed out to me several times the past couple of years, a rough log-hewn cape, is just up the road, across from the water, in the direction we had been heading.

"It's just beautiful here," I tell Richard. Which it is. He nods. The sun is shining on the rocks across the water. The air is fresh and sweet.

Richard says, "Follow me and we'll go up to my 'other' place—that's where the lilacs are." He gets in his truck without a word to the young man who is still standing by the side of the road, turns around, and heads back the way we came.

We turn into a steep, gravelly, rutted drive in about half a mile, heading in what appears to me to be nearly straight up. After a couple of hundred feet, the road levels to a parking area next to a very strange structure resembling nothing so much as a prison sentry tower. A square wooden building, probably 15'x15', the tower is composed of two such cubes sitting atop one another, slightly askew. The top cube is nearly all glass, like a lookout. The roof is slightly slanted, and a stove pipe sticks out. The whole thing is rough lumber, unpainted. The building looks like a child's drawing of a tower. It's obvious, without even going inside, that the view is spectacular. Even from the driveway, we are looking down on Mud Pond, which curves away to the west. All around this structure, all around the "dooryard," are found items: junk cars, lumber, bricks, piles of stones, gas cans, tools. Parked between a couple of trees further up the hill is a small Kubota tractor.

Behind the tower is a clearing where a stand of lilacs is planted in perfectly straight rows, probably thirty trees set four feet apart, all about eight feet tall. The trees are bursting with buds and absolutely beautifully shaped. The pruning job is superb. Their orientation on the hillside places them facing south-southwest. The woods and continuing hillside behind protect them from northerly winds.

Up here in the clear air, the lilacs receive lovely pollinating breezes and sweet warm sunshine, especially in spring before the trees above leaf out. The limey clay soil drains down the drive. It's a textbook lilac garden in this zone, at this latitude: the genus *syringa perfectus*.

Richard is already out of his truck. He's a compact, wiry man, with curls of wispy gray hair brushing his collar beneath a faded blue bandanna, tied over the top of his head, biker style. He's wearing a faded tee shirt under an open flannel shirt, and jeans, work boots. I will see that this is Richard's standard outfit, always the kerchief, jeans, and boots. His glasses are smoked, changing between clouded and dark as the sun chases in and out, but never lightening to clear.

Despite the stained teeth, he does not appear to smoke. Ed says he probably does pot. He looks rough but not unclean. His clothes are old and faded but not dirty.

He likes being complimented on the lilacs. Ed had told me that Bernard always called Richard rough, always criticized the work Richard did in the garden, but it is obvious that Richard's treatment of these lilacs is masterful. The trees are splendid specimens, splendidly cared for. When asked if these trees came from the garden, he smiles. "Of course," he says. Ed asks him if he's going to take more plants. "I don't need to," Richard says, "I got 'em all."

We lean against the truck and talk a little about his growing up. I tell him some of the things his cousin John Kelleher told me, that Bernard was hard on him. Richard does his little bowing dance. "Yesss," he says. I tell him John asked to be remembered to him, and he says, "I always liked John." Like John, he agrees that Bernard and his sister Laura Kelleher were two peas in a pod. "Get those two together and watch out."

"I guess they were both critical," I begin and Richard suddenly looks up hard at me.

"Bernard was a gentleman," Richard says. "He was a refined man."

Ed asks, "Are you being sarcastic?"

"No I'm not," Richard says matter-of-factly. He says he just didn't fit in, that Bernard and Rena were too old. "The first thing I did when I arrived in that house was to break a fancy dish," Richard says, bowing. That can't be right. He was an infant when he went to live with them, but it is the essence of their relationship; it's how he remembers it, and in that sense, an apt characterization. He and Bernard just did not see eye to eye.

"See, I was different," Richard says, and it is obvious that he has

For the son of middle-class parents, he has shockingly bad teeth, stained brown and crooked. His long, lantern face is lined, gaunt, and his hands are work worn. He has a habit of bending from the waist forward and kicking one foot out in front of him, toe up, as though he were about to launch into a dance, like an ancient kokopelli. He does it when he's said something he thinks is shocking. Or true. His whole body ripples with his language. He bends over, sticks out his foot, and rocks back before straightening up. He bends often and plucks at a piece of grass. These are self-effacing postures. It's hard to imagine him indoors.

I say something about being stiff and the vicissitudes of old age as I climb out of the truck, and Richard stops and looks at me sharply. "Not for a Buddhist," he says. "I'm just passing through. Always another body." Ed will say later that Richard is a very spiritual man. I'm not attuned to those things, but he certainly does seem true to himself.

We admire the lilacs, which are beautifully kept. Richard nods. Apparently there are no secrets in the Oxford shire. He seems to know that Ed has been volunteering down at the garden this morning, helping Kristin the horticulturist prune lilacs.

"What are they doing down there?" he asks Ed. "Why are they pruning now? Don't they know they won't have any flowers next month?" Ed says that they have a plan to try to bring some of the trees back for another year, about how they've gotten too tall.

"Way too tall," Richard says. "Bernard always said six to eight feet."

"I say eight to ten feet," Ed says, "but you could be right."

"Yes I am," says Richard. Richard has a way of speaking directly. He makes clear statements and waits for your reaction. He asks questions like "what are they doing?" Not "what do you think?" He is well spoken with a country accent. No profanity. Good grammar.

liked being different all his life even though it has caused him a lot of trouble. He has embraced his differentness. And he could not be more different, outwardly, from Bernard McLaughlin, who was, as Richard says, a gentleman. "They made me take piano lessons," he says, bowing and weaving, his bobbing to the memory. "Four years. Every chance I got, I was out the window, out someplace else." The billiard room and table were right next to his bedroom, and he perfected his game. By the time he was in his early teens, he could hustle pool. He climbed out the window at night, sliding down Bernard's famous tricolor beech. Later, in his thirties, he earned a living as a pool shark both in Virginia and Connecticut.

He laughs about going to New York after he and Bernard had a "dust up." "Bernard had to come and get me," he says. "I was fifteen." I ask him about that, about what Bernard said on that long drive back to Maine. "He didn't say a word," says Richard. "The police chief came because I had to be brought back by 'an officer of the law,' and Bernard had to come with him, but he didn't want to be there, and he didn't say a word. After that they put me right away into St. Francis in Biddeford. I lasted about two months. After that I was in and out of Bridgton Academy and Paris High. I enlisted and went to Germany at eighteen and I never looked back. Later I went down to Virginia in some bow tournaments. Went down to Connecticut and lived there for a while."

The McLaughlin relatives cluck about Richard, about how "difficult" he was. His cousin John Kelleher, whose mother Laura was Bernard's oldest sister, thought Bernard and Rena were harsh with Richard. "There was nothing he could do right," John recalled. While he has fond memories of spending his childhood summers with the other McLaughlin cousins at the "farm," as his grandfather Will

McLaughlin's house in Limestone was called, he has no recollection that Richard was ever there. "I don't even remember Uncle Bernard being there," John said. "We always saw him at his house in South Paris," where, John also remembered, Richard was "always in hot water."

In a feature story, "Seeds of Discontent," published in the Lewiston *Sun Journal* on September 25, 1996, Susan Rayfield painted this picture: "Richard McLaughlin, 59, doesn't get along with people much. His very appearance—camouflage cap and bandanna, spider belt buckle, right forearm tattooed with 'death before dishonor'—spells rebel." She quotes Richard as saying " '[Bernard] tried to make something out of me but it wouldn't stick. He wanted me to be an upstanding citizen, with a good education and a nice job. You push me and I go the opposite direction. That's all I can say.' "

Richard neither confirms nor denies this account. He just nods. "Well," he says, "you read it in the paper. Must be true." He does verify that he used the $10,000 he inherited when Rena died in 1981 to buy a junkyard in the nearby town of Oxford (that he still owns and operates), and to travel to India and Nepal for three months to gain "an attitude adjustment." Richard confirms that he came back from that trip a Buddhist and committed to a rapprochement with his father. "Seemed time to work things out," is his only comment. To some extent he must have achieved this, for from the mid-1980s on, Richard worked in the garden, mowing, weeding, what he calls "caretaking." When Ed asked Bernard to take him on a day a week as an apprentice in the late 1980s, Richard was working there. Ed recalls that Bernard prepared lunch for the three of them. Ed says father and son were "cordial but not warm."

"Oh, he was all right," Richard says to this recollection. "He was tough. It can't have been easy for him." When asked about the courtship of his adoptive parents, whether he knows why, if they were sweethearts since college as some have suggested, they waited until Rena was forty-two to marry, Richard says, "The old sea captain thought he was a gold digger. After her father died, Rena stayed on with her mother. It wasn't until her mother died that Rena was free to marry." The way he says this, even the language—*free to marry*—sounds like the kind of oft-told family script handed down through the years. I don't push Richard on this point because it seems that, like most children, he doesn't really know how it was between his parents when he was young. What he does have a sense of, however, are the Tribous, his mother's family.

"Where's the old sea captain down there?" Richard asks, gesturing downhill in the direction of South Paris, in the direction of his family home. "All I see is 'Bernard' this and 'Bernard' that. I don't see anything about the history of the Tribous. I'm a Tribou. That land belonged to my family. Rena told me that when Bernard passed, the farm would come to me, that it would stay in the family. That didn't happen, did it?"

I tell him that the Foundation had an intern recently who spent half the summer researching the Tribou family, tracking down the ships his grandfather had skippered, poking around graveyards in Bucksport and Machias, along the coast downeast where Richard was born.

"There's a whole drawer full of ship's logs and manifests, of lists of Tribou family trees," I tell him.

He laughs. "Show all the bad apples?" he asks. He's been talking a long time, stepping from foot to foot, bending down and plucking weeds from around the iris and peony gardens next to the lilacs. He's standing next to me now. We're about the same height, the same age. Some high weather clouds have blown in, and we can feel a chill.

His smoked lenses have lightened. He stands up straight and looks right at me.

"It's all over," he says quietly. "It's all done with now. But what matters are my kids. I don't care about all that other stuff. But that's my kids' family home. My boys should be caretaking down there. My grandkids should be able to walk around that house and see where their granddad grew up." He bends once and then stands up straight. "That's what it's all about."

V.

It is Memorial Day 2002 in the McLaughlin Garden, the third day of the Lilac Festival, a sweet, warm May day, clear, a little breezy. Maybe fifty people are circulating through the four-acre garden, renowned for its heirloom lilacs, some of which no longer bloom in any other place. They walk slowly, following the assigned paths past the grand avenue of lilacs nodding above them, now a little overgrown, at least fourteen feet to the prescribed six to eight Bernard always favored. It's been a cold spring, so the lilacs are not quite to their peak. Some have opened, but they haven't had the hot sun to really plump them out, coax the full heady fragrance, unfurl the starlike clusters of perfect tiny blooms. Even so, at least half of this group carries notebooks, peers at the blossoms above, sniffs at those down low, and makes notes.

Beyond the lilacs, near the barn, are the hosta and perennial gardens, stunning this time of year in dappled light under the early citreous leaves of overstoreying oaks and maples. Ferns bright as Granny Smith apples, three feet high and full of spunk, climb the slope beyond. The lady slippers are missing now, but *myostosis*, the uncommonly blue forget-me-not, dazzles on all sides as well as up the hill. In their airy bloom, the forget-me-nots are cerulean like the spring sky: boundless yet insubstantial; deep yet soft. They nestle like clouds under the shrubs and around the rocks, a promise the color of heaven. The daffodils and tulips have mostly gone by, and the irises have not yet come on. Still the garden charms this soft spring morning.

Behind the barn, a magnificent hand-hewn hemlock structure now prominently ensconced, along with the house and the garden itself on the National Register of Historic Places, Dan Lakeman is setting up his station at the open end of a semicircle of old wooden chairs and garden benches. An interpretative reader who has performed *Peter and the Wolf* with the Portland (Maine) Symphony Orchestra, Lakeman is here for his third annual reading of Walt Whitman's "When Lilacs Last in the Dooryard Bloom'd," an event much heralded by the McLaughlin Foundation. A neat, contained man in his fifties, Lakeman is dapper in khakis, a blue checked shirt, and jaunty burgundy bow tie. He sets up a music stand with his text, a small bench alongside with his glasses, bottles of Poland Spring water, and a book of Emily Dickinson's poems.

People drift in through the barn, settle on the old chairs. They ask each other if they've been here before, who Lakeman is, and what is going to happen. The Foundation circular lists him as "Maine's Own Dan Lakeman." A woman with binoculars asks the man in front of her if Lakeman is an actor. He doesn't know.

The day could not be more perfect. It vibrates with light and fragrance, yet its essence is tranquility. Birds swoop and shrill overhead, caroling from one side of the garden to the other. Sunlight breaks through the leaves, spotlighting exactly the circle on the grass where Lakeman soon will stand. He comes out of the barn and goes to the end of the nearest path, calling to people in the garden that the reading is about to begin if they care to join the group. He walks to his makeshift podium. No one presents him.

"We're a little short of staff today," he smiles. "The Director is manning the gift shop." He introduces himself, says he's an interpretative reader, and then speaks quite eloquently about the ways in which war has made itself apparent in our world today, even here in this idyllic setting. Probably thirty people are now circled around him. He makes the obvious analogy to 9-11, how until then Memorial Day had become just another holiday. He reminds us it is so much different now. He draws us into the knowledge of Whitman's patriotism, compares it to our own so recently renewed, and pulls us up to Lincoln.

He warms up the crowd with two short but right-on Dickinson poems. She's a poet, he smiles, he has recently "rediscovered." Emily Dickinson is good for this group. She's immediate, and "Perhaps you'd like to buy a flower," giving a nod to the garden, is greeted with smiles. "I'll tell you how the sun rose … a ribbon at a time" is brilliantly chosen, keeping the tone in tune with the scene while shifting the mood perceptibly to a universally understood metaphor for life and death, the rising and setting sun, light and darkness. In this fragrant garden just off Western Avenue in South Paris, Maine, more than thirty people are sitting up, leaning forward, rapt, as a man stands before them in a spill of sunshine, reading poetry.

Lakeman has done his homework on Whitman. He is careful to point out the three central unifying symbols in this poem, often identified by scholars as the finest elegy in American literature: the western star, the wood thrush, and the lilac. He provides a brushstroke explication without belaboring the point. It is a measure of how well he understands his audience, realizing their lack of familiarity with the nuts and bolts of literary criticism while acknowledging their inherent ability to recognize truth and beauty when they hear it, even in language as baroque as Whitman's. He reminds us of the funeral cortège winding past the lilac-overhung dooryards of the Middle West as the train bore Lincoln's body from Washington home to Illinois for burial.

Just as Lakeman is about to begin reading, a man next door to the McLaughlin Garden, about fifty yards away, beyond the big stone wall, fires up his riding lawnmower. The lovely calm, the travel back in time, is shattered. We are jerked from the dusty sidings where the black train rolled to discourteous present-day America. Lakeman gives a generous smile.

"We've got a little competition," he says, and notches up his voice. Because he is a trained reader, he is able to keep his pace and timing and focus. He does not let the disruption rule. The audience, however, is noticeably discomfited. A woman on the side nearest the offending mower keeps looking over her shoulder and whispering to her companion, a man who looks like he does not want to become involved. A couple of people in the back get up, pace behind their chairs, and throw sour glances to the neighbor. He's an older man, heavyset, wearing an old fishing hat as he circles, vindictively it seems, around and around in the same thirty-foot area right next to the stone wall dividing his land from the garden. Beyond him, way on the other side of his yard, are huge areas of unmowed grass, yet he circles, spins the wheel, edges right along the wall, circles back, and goes over the same ground again. From time to time he looks up at the group in the garden but, as is often the way with a person completely focused on a task at hand, his attention appears to be centered not on how he might be disturbing this assembly but rather on why they are all collected there. It seems possible, on his fourth pass along the stone wall, that this may even be why he persists in this area. He's trying to figure out what's happening.

Lakeman soldiers on. It is magnificent how, in this very difficult situation, he does not give in. His presentation is studied, careful, and builds beautifully. He has a couple of repetitive hand gestures that anchor and reorient the listener. Palm flat and flexed forward for darkness and death. Palm open and lifting for the western star. His body is taut, uncoiling with the rhythms of the language; but his face is mobile, relaxed. It is obvious he has been trained vocally to open up his range and resonance by keeping those muscles loose. By sheer will and expertise, he holds the audience. This is a long poem, sixteen stanzas, at least fifteen minutes in the reading, and halfway through, Lakeman has his group back. There are still a couple of pacers in the back, glaring back and forth between Lakeman and the mower, but for the most part, the power and beauty of the language and cadence have triumphed. All eyes are on Lakeman.

And then, as though on cue, just as Lakeman reads "Lo, the most excellent sun so calm and haughty," the mower turns, rolls away across the length of his property and disappears behind a barn. Fading. Fading. Gone. Lakeman does not miss a beat. A bird that could even be a thrush trills out overhead. The ferns dance and sparkle on the hillside behind him. "The gentle soft-born measureless light."

When he finishes, the famous "Lilac and star and bird twined with the chant of my soul / There in the fragrant pines and the cedars dusk and dim," there is a burst of truly heartfelt applause, joined even by a few stragglers from the garden who have come in late and gathered to stand in the back, slowed and silenced by this homage to God and country, bird and tree.

A small group clusters around Lakeman, sharing with him memories of other poems they've heard and loved, how and where they learned them. It is possible, hearing this, seeing the response he has elicited, to believe there is a thirst in the land for the truth and beauty of language. Lakeman says that the most rewarding aspect of this experience for him is turning people on to poetry. He says that so many people have told him they went out and bought a book of poems after hearing him read. He recounts how local bookstores were sold out of a particular volume after one of his performances. He's not bragging. He's touched and moved. Formerly an accountant, he is now, in late middle age, in residence with his wife at the Bangor Theological Seminary, studying for the ministry. He says he would like to bring more poetry, even more than is in the gospels, to the pulpit.

The effect of his reading is pervasive. The cadences resonate in the air, matching the fragrant breezes, the birdsong, and even our bodies' rhythms. We seem to have been centered and put in our places. There is a softness and measure to the crowd moving away from the reading.

It is nearly noon now, and the sun beats straight down, pulling at the garden. Standing on the grassy path between the perfumed, bowing lilacs, Lakeman is illuminated in a scene that could have been caught in the sepia lens of a daguerreotype. Indeed, everything about this setting, the old wooden chairs, Lakeman in his checkered shirt and bow tie, even the old neighbor mowing, harkens to another, better time. In her introduction to Sanford Phippen's *The Messiah in the Memorial Gym*, publisher, poet and University of Maine professor Constance Hunting wrote:

> I call 'rural wonder,' the disproportionate awe with which one

regards a quite ordinary event or circumstance, elevating it to near-sacred status. Rural wonder often depends on saw or platitude, death to art. By all means admire your vase of simple flowers; but set it on the window sill so that it may look out at and be looked back at by the universal landscape.

In the midst of terrorism and scandal in the church, there has been an uplifting moment in the garden Bernard McLaughlin created. I am trying to keep my own "rural wonder" in check, to put this scene into not only my own perspective but also into the larger picture of the proprietary interests at play here. I am trying to put Memorial Day in the McLaughlin Garden up on a big open window sill. I have been shaken, however, by both the performance and the response it elicited. I wonder how Richard would have felt.

And I cannot help but see this scene as a reenactment of the tensions and cultural dichotomies that tore this splendid place asunder only a few years earlier. The disparity between today's serenity and the turmoil jars me. In the sweet sunshine, the garden suddenly seems to me as it was the first time I saw it several years earlier: shadowy and dormant; peopled by dark forces. Am I one of them? A pretender here? Lakeman and his audience and the old neighbor mowing represent the factions who believe they each embody the "right" use of this geography. Inside, "manning the gift shop," is Lee Dassler, who has been generous and open to me. I have not become a part of the story, but the story has become part of me, and certain unauthorized aspects have taken hold. Only a few days earlier, six years after the Foundation bought the property, Richard McLaughlin had told me, in reference to the upcoming Lilac Festival, "I'm going to rain on their parade. Wait till you see what we've got planned." Like Lee Dassler before me, I find myself looking up to the ridge.

Standing on the path that Memorial Day, I wonder what the old gardener would have made of it all: the poetry reading, the gift shop, the ladies from bus tours eating salads with nasturtiums from his garden off his Fiesta Ware on his old sun porch.

VI.

Early on, Lee Dassler asked me to provide a statement of the scope of my work for inclusion in the Foundation newsletter. This is what she published from the information I gave her:

> She sees Bernard's life as a mirror of 20th century rural accomplishment and is framing the work as a history-biography, spanning the years from the turn-of-the-century in Limestone to finish with the mid- and end-century in South Paris. 'His garden,' she says, is a perfect metaphor for the peculiarly American notion of the good life gained through hard work.

She doesn't say that she told me I couldn't mention Richard. Otherwise, that's what I told her. The difficulty for me has become my burgeoning awareness of the difference between the way in which the people associated with the McLaughlin Foundation and the locals perceive not only its "reality," but also its significance. I cannot separate those differing perceptions from the life of Bernard McLaughlin.

Many writers have addressed the perils facing the biographer. One discussed the "wrenching relationships between biographer and subject." Wrenching resonates. Maine writer Sanford Phippen notes in his essay "The People of Winter":

> Those who dream of Maine—as opposed to, say, California—tend to see it not as presenting a life of ease but as a simplification. Some of the well-fixed summer or retired folk

> with well-insulated homes with pictures windows framing Currier and Ives views do manage to have their Maine just as simple as they anticipated. But ... poorer people are confronted with ... [a] Maine [that] is cold, dark and often deformed, recognizable not in the sunny seascapes of so many Sunday painters. ... This Maine is frustrating; it is hard on people.

It is the "simplification" of the McLaughlin Garden story that confounds me, the "sunny" landscape which does not allow for Richard pacing darkly on the ridge.

History is always revisionist, always under construction, and landscapes shift, now sifting over this, now laying bare that. When I asked Michael DesPlaines, the new Director of the Foundation after Lee Dassler's resignation in 2005, whether they still had any "trouble" with Richard, DesPlaines remarked, "I don't even know what he looks like. That's ancient history." I asked Judith Meyers what would have happened if Richard had "gotten" the garden rather than the Foundation. She smiled at that question and took her time in answering. Finally she said, "Well, the garden would be perfect— much better than it is today. And the house and the barn would have fallen apart."

When I was down at the Norway Historical Society in the summer of 2003, I asked Guy Campbell, the curator, if he knew about Bernard's garden. The two towns are less than a minute apart.

"Well," he answered, "'course I heard about them. They're just gardens. Not much different from anyone else's." The day before, when I'd called to make an appointment with him to open up the archive for me, he'd answered on a cell phone from out in his own garden where he was "burning" Japanese beetles with an acetylene torch.

"Most people put them in a can of gasoline," I'd offered.

"This is faster," Mr. Campbell answered, a man in his mid-eighties who doesn't have time to waste. "Gets 'em right good."

Now, in the archive, I asked him if he'd heard about the *Altogether for the Garden* nude calendar, Lee Dassler's most successful fund-raising project, which features Board members undressed in the garden.

"Heard something about that," he allowed.

"But you haven't seen it?"

"Oh no, why would I want to see it?"

The Foundation had been able to retire its mortgage, I told him, on sales of the calendar. He clucked. "Some people will buy anything."

I attended a talk on winter gardens sponsored by the Foundation in January, one of the series of programs they run to keep up year-round interest. Susan Carter, a landscape architect from Gnome, an upscale coastal firm that has moved more granite around Maine than the glaciers, was showing slides of "natural" stone walls. A group of Paris Hill matrons was absorbed in the slides, balancing china teacups on their knees.

Afterwards, I talked to Kristin Perry, the horticulturalist, who has settled into the rigors of a single life in rural Maine—after a tough start—and is now prospering at the Foundation. She's earnest and hard working, a very knowledgeable young woman who has effected wonderful improvements in the garden. We were admiring the beautiful architect's drawings which are framed in each of the downstairs rooms showing how they might look if restored (an "adopt-a-room" project Lee Dassler instituted) when the current president of the board came over to inquire as to the progress of "our book."

"These things take time," I hedged, and then directed her attention to the drawing Kristin and I had been examining. It was of the dining room, the room in which the talk had just been given, and featured an enormous brass and crystal chandelier.

"Was that actually in this house?" I asked her. "Somehow it doesn't seem to fit Bernard's style."

She rolled her eyes. "Who knows?" she said with umbrage. "He took everything. Stripped the rooms. You wouldn't believe."

"Richard?" I asked.

"Who else?" she said, touching my arm as though we were in this together.

It had been a dream of mine, once I got to know Richard McLaughlin and realized that not only had he not destroyed the files or the plants or the Iris Society winning ribbons but that he had lovingly maintained them all to effect a rapprochement of my own. I would have liked to convince Richard to let the Foundation buy them from him so that they could have the records they needed, and he could let go of his anger. The reporter Judy Meyers laughed when she heard that.

"Never happen," she said. "They mean too much to him." She was right. "Richard," she told me, "is a man to whom many promises have been made. All his life. And not many of them have been kept. And don't forget," she added, "he's not angry. He has forgiven them. He's just hurt."

One of Richard's biggest grievances with the Foundation was over their handling of his son Tony's request to be married there. The McLaughlin Garden has become a popular place for weddings. The Foundation has a special brochure describing this service they offer.

Their brochure states that no weddings can be scheduled during the month of May because that is peak lilac season, and the time of the Lilac Festival. Tony wanted to be married on Mother's Day. Lee turned him down. No weddings in May. See, it says so right here. Richard was furious.

When I broached this subject to Lee, she was visibly upset. She kept waving the brochure in my face and saying, "Do they think I would have a brochure printed up just to deny them?"

Judy Meyers said, "Don't you think the one exception the Foundation could have made to that rule was for Bernard McLaughlin's grandson?"

Lee said, "These are the rules."

At the end of the summer I went looking for Richard at the "museum" he had started the year before. The narrow white building is located at the end of a residential street in Norway, just a few minutes from the McLaughlin Garden. It looks like a trailer, but the structure was probably a food shack of some kind that Richard transported there. Wooden steps lead up to a door on the narrow end, and inside are counters under windows running along both long sides. I hadn't been there since more than a year earlier, the spring when Richard was just setting it up, just getting his "real McLaughlin Museum" ready to rain on the Lilac Festival parade. Then, the countertops had been heaped with yellow and blue and purple Iris Society ribbons. Pictures of the McLaughlin family homestead in Limestone and the original Tribou house in South Paris hung on the walls. Today, the building is empty, and all the McLaughlin memorabilia is gone. The shack was jacked up on stumps.

I walked around it. The steps were gone, and it was obvious the operation was shut down. I was just about to get back in my car and leave when a man came running down the driveway next door, carrying a shovel and wiping his brow in the heat. He looked vaguely familiar, but I did not know him.

"Hey," he called to me. "Aren't you the writer lady?"

"That's right," I answered.

"I'm Walter," he said sticking out his hand. "I'm Walter Bressette. I'm so glad to finally meet you. Hey," he looked behind to where a young man was coming down the driveway slowly. I recognized him as the same young man who had been talking to Richard by the side of the road the first time I met Richard. "You know Tony, don't you? This is Richard's son. This is Tony." Walter pushed him forward and Tony shook my hand firmly.

"Well, whatta think?" Walter said, gesturing to the shack. "We got her all jacked up and we've built a foundation up the hill. Gonna be a real museum. Gonna be the real thing." He beamed at me. "Did you see Richard's lilacs this year?" he asked. I said unfortunately I had not. "Oh they were something. Weren't they something, Tony? Oh my God. They were some beautiful."

Hunting By Permission

I was fifty-four and widowed five years the first time I answered a personal ad. My children had moved out, my career choices were uninteresting, my passion had vanished. I could only look backward, not forward. I could only imagine who I had been, not who I might become.

A personal ad seemed unthinkable to me, but all my friends said "it was done," and especially in Portland, Maine, such a small, safe city. The one I circled read "Divorced white male enjoys nature, literature, sunsets, sunrises, fine dining, travel. Seeking interesting, intelligent single/divorced female with similar interests." In hindsight, this was an unusual choice for me. It seems I hedged my bets. All the men in my life had been intellectual, creative, and Jewish, urban. Men who had taken me up and out of the Midwest where I had come of age, my blue gentile eyes always seeking the horizon across its vast safe, uninteresting flatness. Men who had brought me to the coast, the edge of America, brought me to where the Atlantic washed ashore from foreign lands and glacial stones pushed up out of the untilled soil. They were men from the city, men to whom the silence of the plains was unknown, men who thrived on the sound of their own voices. But I had lapsed from them into my silent celibacy. Without even knowing it, I went looking for a man of few words, a man of action, not thought.

As it turned out, Peter did indeed love nature, sunsets, sunrises. Literature to him meant seafaring adventures of the seventeenth century; fine dining was any meal prepared by another person; and after a youth in the Navy and Merchant Marines when he must have enjoyed travel, by this time in his life he rarely went outside the bounds of his considerable property in Limington, Maine.

The words caught my eye, but Peter's voice pulled me in. These were "voice" personals. If you liked what you read, you could, for a price, dial a number and hear a recorded message by the same person; and then, if you liked, leave a message yourself. Peter was well spoken, but when I heard him describe walking in the woods of Limington with his dog, it was not his style nor even his choice of words, but rather the timbre of his deep, dark voice that spoke to me.

The night in June I called and left a message for him was Cape Fun Days at Fort Williams Park, just down the street from my home on the coast near Portland. In the evening, after the clowns and face painters and kite flyers had gone, the children were treated to fireworks over the ocean. As I sat in my study, I watched the sparks and flares of dying bursts through my window. The sound of fireworks filled the air. Boom.

Peter didn't return my call for over a week. It turned out he had more than forty responses from women who wanted a nature-loving man. Always cautious, he had listened to each several times and rejected all but mine. Like me, he also didn't heed the written word. In the end, my carefully scripted statement of how I might suit him didn't catch his interest: it was the sound of cannon fire in the background. Boom.

After our initial telephone exchange, Peter agreed to come to my house on a Sunday afternoon near the end of June. I was filling saucers with beer to lure slugs out of the gardens. Peter drove up in a beautiful bronze 1979 Mercedes SEL convertible, one of those big chrome models. When he stepped out from behind the wheel, I knew I was in for a different sort of man: six feet with muscular and tanned legs and arms. His waist was trim, nipped in with a woven leather belt under a broad chest and wide shoulders. He wore khaki shorts and a pink, short-sleeved Oxford shirt, white socks, and boating shoes. A neatly trimmed white beard and mustache and short white hair completed this man, who looked like all the men I had seen on the docks of yacht clubs in New England. All those men easy in their bodies who were harder for me to approach than the men I knew who could be won by words. Athletic and loose. Privileged and casual. I stood there with a bottle of Heineken and a saucer, awkward in my gardening clothes.

"Penelope?" he asked. "What are you doing?" he continued before even confirming my name. "That's good beer!"

"Oh, it's left over from my daughter's graduation party," I said, feeling foolish. "You must be Peter," I continued, although I knew instantly who he was from his deep voice. He smiled, a beautiful smile with even white teeth, like an actor.

"None other," he said. "Do you have any of that cold?" And, once I put down the beer, he shook my hand firmly. "So this is how they do it in Cape Elizabeth," he laughed. "Premium beer for the bugs. My my." He leaned against his car and looked me up and down. I was flustered. I wasn't used to such frank appraisal. A couple of important facts about Peter were set before me that summer afternoon. He exuded a very physical presence and was a man's man. He, and his whole family, as it turned out, collected vintage automobiles. He came on with the charm of a salesman. And he liked his drink.

You could be licensed to hunt nearly all the time in Limington, Maine, a township in the foothills of the Western Mountains, thirty miles northwest of Cape Elizabeth. I didn't know that the first time I drove out there to see Peter, a week after our initial meeting. Although it only took me an hour, it was a trip backwards in terms of culture, from coastal Maine's polished gentility to up-country roughness. Stuck between the mighty Saco River to the east and the New Hampshire border to the west, Limington township is a modern rural sprawl of trailers and convenience stores fronting land that once boasted proud farms. Only the town hall and a village green designate its center. It's one of those places in present-day back-country America where there is no "there" there. In Limington, as in many rural areas, hunting stands in for a collective historical consciousness, a confirmation of the time when founding fathers were resourceful and resilient. At the center of that self-reliance is an intrinsic melancholy seeping out of the forest, that shadowy place of wild things and uncontrolled growth.

I didn't know any of that either the Sunday afternoon I first saw Peter's land. Or I couldn't have articulated it. I just felt uneasiness as I left the coast behind me and penetrated further into a vista of abandoned rusting cars, handmade signs advertising home businesses to sharpen saws, repair TVs, cut hair. The roads I traveled grew narrower and narrower until finally I was on a nearly single-lane tract, the Boothby Road. Consulting the long list of turns and signposts I had written on a sheet of yellow legal paper, I saw that ahead on my right, just beyond a large granite boulder, I would see a drive heading in, marked by an open gate. A green and gold medallion sign swung from a big oak just inside the gate: "TREE FARM Firewood ◆ Christmas Trees ◆ Field Stone." On my left, open meadows sloped down to the Little Ossipee River, shining through willows on the bank. I turned up the drive, its center marked by foothigh daisies billowing under my axle. It wound a quarter mile uphill, passing several falling-down old barns, then widened and crested on a ridge covered with wild roses and autumn olive.

In front of me spread what would become my world for the next three years. Just below was a pond more than three acres wide, a huge sparkling body of water. It was surrounded by soft green sedge, which made the sides appear mossy and sweet, accessible. Beyond, directly across the pond from the drive, a terraced hillside of balsam fir marched in measured rows, their symmetry emphasizing control and accomplishment, rigor wrested out of the forest. At the west end of the pond, to my left, an impressive waterway dam—more than ten feet across—further demonstrated Peter's dominion over this property. At the other end of the pond, an arched, rustic bridge crossed Nat Leach Brook, which flowed out of wider water and up into the woods. And just before that, situated not thirty feet from the edge of the water, was a building that looked to me like a hunting lodge, post-and-beam pillars supporting a shingled roof, a huge stone chimney marking one side. Peter stood in front of this structure, waving me in, a huge grin covering his face. This was his kingdom. He wanted me to see it all.

Eventually I did. Eventually I came to know every foot of Peter's more than two hundred acres. To the exclusion of nearly everything else. During the three years I lived in Limington, we hardly went off that property. In the beginning, Peter drove me down all the logging roads first on his four-wheeler and then, when the snow came, on a snowmobile. I literally took to the woods. I had grown up with nature, but it had been many years since I had spent so much time smelling and looking and listening, since I had learned the names of trees and watched the seasons spin through. Since I had heard the silence.

Deer hunting season is a big event in rural Maine. People who don't do any other kind of hunting gear up to "get their deer." Coming as it does for the entire month of November, deer season bridges the times of productive harvest and dormant winter, providing an appropriately sanguine transition. Figures in blaze orange replace the fading, flaming foliage. The impending solstice adds urgency. The sky lowers. More than a sport, deer hunting takes on the aspect of an annual and sacred ritual, not just a rite of passage of both men and season but also a restatement of the enduring and complicated relationship between the land and its stewards.

Although no discernible anti-hunting sentiment was evident in Limington, disputes about land use and the posting and restricting of land were common. Peter's two-hundred-acre tree farm had been the sometime camp of a family who lived out of town when he bought it twenty years earlier. The locals had long been using it as their own. Rather than post the land against hunting, Peter had put up Hunting By Permission Only signs. It was an inspired compromise. He knew who was on the land, and more important, where they were hunting. He had a sign-in log posted in a wooden box on the side of the barn. Hunters spoke to Peter before the season began and he told them the rules: they had to sign in and out, had to let him know how many were in the party and where they were on the farm. It was a beautiful system. The log book told him how many deer were taken, even how many deer were sighted. It became a kind of hunters' diary, entries scrawled in rough pencil of how the day had gone, touching notes of wildlife sightings: "That three-legged spike is still up at the Oakes. Looks stronger this year." "Saw a flock of wild turkeys in the old plantation." "Watch them coyotes. Saw a female with a pup in The Pines, right near the house."

The notion of Peter's tree farm being an entity unto itself was emphasized by the signs he had erected all over the property. Cut from oak he had milled himself off the land, the signs were three feet by eight inches, all painted the Tree Farm green and gold, and nailed to trees. Peter routed out their signage in his workshop in the barn: The Oakes (a stand of hundred-year-old trees on a ridge on the northern boundary); The Pines (a four-acre stand of trees set at regular intervals above the pond); the Cuckoo's Nest (a tree stand used exclusively by his friend Dr. Luigi Cuchoo). It was like living in a Richard Scarry book. But the signs also lent credibility, an essence to the property. (They also helped me when I lost my way.) When his hunting-by-permission men left notes, they always identified exactly where they had been by using the names from those signs.

I grew up in Northern Michigan in the 1940s in a family that hunted and depended on what could be grown or caught or killed. Though I never hunted, I tagged along with my grandfather as he shot snow geese and rabbits, even the occasional deer. I knew that most hunters honor the animals that gave their lives, in the same way farmers who butcher their stock go about the task with a certain dignity. But like the woods, I hadn't thought about hunting in years. Until I saw Peter bow his head and softly touch the breast of a grouse he shot. I'd seen my grandfather do the same thing.

The excitement of deer hunting season is infectious, a rustle in the air, a sense of expectancy, and I am caught up in its urgency. The local grange serves a hunters' breakfast beginning at three on the morning the season opens. Women begin cooking just after midnight. By two thirty, the parking lot is full, and clouds of frosty breath float in the yellow light that spills from the tall windows.

At Peter's house, we have coffee and oatmeal ready on the wood stove for the hunters who are joining us this morning. These men fill the room with their fresh woolly smell from outdoors. Like us, they are dressed in layers of long winter underwear and wool sweaters over neoprene overalls, two pairs of socks and high boots. As if the deer might hear us, we all speak in hushed tones. No one sits down. The guns are stacked outside the back door, thermoses filled with coffee. I am very excited, but I keep on the edge of this group, feeling my presence as a woman an impediment to the bonding. The men are very serious.

No shot can be fired before sunup, but hunters need to be in position long before that time. Even though the deer are moving around more now than normally—as the bucks are rutting, looking for does in estrus—they still follow the habit of feeding at night and returning to rest in the early morning. The process is reversed at dusk. We have been scouting their movements. On Peter's land, deer trails are fairly well established. The herd sleeps under cedar trees down in low hollows during the day and travels up the ridges to feed on apples and clover at night.

We head out about four thirty. The men agree who will go where. Since the land belongs to Peter, he announces first where we will be. The others, two groups of two each, start away from us in different directions, one group up the path behind the house toward the western boundary, a stand of spruce in the abandoned tree plantation. The other group walks along the pond in front of the house and straight up through The Pines, a cathedral of tall old trees, evenly spaced and set out on a carpet of needles and duff many inches thick. They fade into the darkness, the glow from their fluorescent orange vests lingering behind them. We go back out the drive, toward the Boothby Road, then up the main logging road around the northern side of the pond, through the old orchard and past the cemetery. Sunup comes at 6:15.

It's thrilling in the frosty early morning, so dark only the gravel reflecting starlight keeps us on track. Soon I can begin to see in the blackness. I feel feral and alert. Crumbling stones glow faintly as we pass the cemetery. I can smell rotting apples along the roadside, then the tang of autumn olive as we head uphill, just above the pond now, behind a ridge of alder. Frost makes the ground hard and silvery underfoot. No snow. We step carefully once we go off the road, but the undergrowth is in that suspended state between being dry and being frozen: pliant, it conforms to our boots and doesn't make a sound. Peter knows a rock where he wants to sit, allowing him to see a spot where two deer trails converge, a little below and in front of him.

This is the part I like best about deer hunting, the settling into the landscape and silent waiting. Peter is a terrific shot, fast and clean, but at sixty-four he doesn't hear well anymore. I have become his ears. I sit a few feet from him, directly in his sight. With hand signals, I indicate where I hear deer. It is in this occasion of known silence that Peter and I interact the best, like when we make love wordlessly and in the dark. We work so well when I know the rules. When I'm not looking for words to define our relationship. So well, that I carry the heat of this success in my heart. My touchstone that yes, I have made the right choice when the silence of this new life overwhelms me. It's what keeps me in Limington.

It takes time to settle into this quiet waiting. At first our clothes, our breathing, even our essence rustle. Each time we have to learn to be still again. By the end of the season, going out twice a day as we will, at dawn and dusk, we will have perfected achieving our stillness quickly, a rhythm I love. But on this first day, we're a little awkward. We wiggle and itch, can't quite get our feet right.

When it comes, it's wonderful. I let myself lean into the rock behind me, relax my shoulders and legs. Dark silence flows over me. All the little life disturbed by our coming rearranges itself. Grasses bend back up. Dirt reforms. Now I can begin to hear the life of the forest. A mouse scurries through leaves somewhere behind me, a scratching sound. With a soft thud, an apple falls from a tree by the road. With a sharp ping, an acorn drops. Way up on the ridge, The Oakes, a fox coughs. Below us, on the pond, a duck skids in with a velvet splash. Beyond the Boothby Road, out on Route 11, a truck downshifts as it approaches the intersection of Route 25.

Light begins to seep in ever so slightly. Some of it is starlight, reflecting off rocks and pale tree trucks. Dark foliage laps the light up eagerly, sucking it away again. When dawn actually does become apparent, it is not by light in the sky so much as by objects obtaining definition, the revenant landscape becoming real. Where there was no color, now there is just sheen of pewter, then brown, then green. Bittersweet berries flush from gray to rose to red, as though they have been brought back to life, color coursing through them.

Soon after I met him, Peter showed me a picture of himself taken at the Stork Club in New York thirty years earlier. It's a great picture: good-sized, substantial, printed on rich creamy stock and mounted in an embossed folder all soft and furred around the edges. The photograph is shot in black and white at an angle. Peter is in the foreground, seated in a leather booth so buttery you can feel yourself slide across its plumped fullness. Beside him is an extraordinarily beautiful young woman, facing the camera but looking adoringly at him. He is turned away from her, full face into the lens, his eyes locked in one of those captured gazes that follow you relentlessly, whichever way you turn. He looks like he knows he is going to pay for this picture.

This couple, young and glamorous and beautiful, live happily ever after in a silent tinkle of good silver against crystal, sweet smoke, and innocent high spirits. You would never need anyone to explain what a nightclub was after balancing the weight of this photograph in your hands. The music swells across the years. This photo says "Let's dance!"

Thirty years later, Peter and I sat at his kitchen table in Limington. I would not have thought this was a man who went to the Stork Club. I could not imagine him dressing in evening clothes, making the effort to mount such an elaborate evening. Except that he had kept this picture. Clean, unbent, it seems to be a treasure offered up, a glimmer brought forth like light years from that faraway starlight roof. A testimony to his romance.

The day he showed me that picture was an unhappy anniversary for Peter. He had spent the morning in court ending his marriage. We didn't mention that, yet I felt a tremor running between these two events, questions unasked and unanswered. No fault. But just that, a deep line running under a life, a loss of sure-footedness. The unseen threat of being torn apart. The inability to prevent it. He didn't say a word but brushed his hand lightly across the photograph, dismissively, as though to dust it. Or wipe it away. Then he looked at it more closely as if he were able to see the future somehow reflected there. His eyes, I noticed, were the same as those in the picture. Amused and careful. Aware of the consequences.

Peter never pretended to be other than what he was: a man of few words who revered the past. That night in the kitchen when he offered up his past, I entered it. No questions. I felt myself settling into a buttery leather booth. The music swelled. I reached across the table and took his hands: Let's dance!

The woods are like the ocean, full of secret currents and eddies. The wind has a life of its own among the trees. Suddenly it will sweep up and past us, turning leaves and lifting boughs. A little dervish, now here, now gone. With dawn, the wind begins to lift ever so slightly. As more color bleeds into the meadow below us, I can smell just a hint of smoke carried up from our woodstove down at the house. A breeze brings me a whiff of cattail on the pond, sour and brown.

Then I hear a sound so delicate it makes me see as well as hear it: a carefully placed cloven hoof set down, just so, between leaves and twigs. The faintest dry rustle. Those fine slender legs. Then another. And another. A deer is approaching us on the far branch of the two paths converging below us. It's not a big deer. There is no sound of branches brushing by its sides as it passes. I signal to Peter by pointing. He is immediately alert, but doesn't lift his gun. It's not first light yet. We both stare intently into the dark before us. I hear a snap, chewing. A bite taken off a passing tree. Probably cedar. Then another step. The deer passes below us behind the alders. For one brief moment, its wide luminous eye catches starlight, just that faint gleam among the branches. Then it moves downhill, steps fading away.

Behind me I hear another deer coming down the path. I can't turn, but I try to move my head, just a little, to hear it better. I signal Peter and he watches intently over my shoulder. Suddenly there is a rifle shot from out on the western boundary. The woods around us explode. The deer leaps away, white tail flashing. Birds cry. Branches flail. One of our hunters has jumped the dawn. It gives us a chance to move, shake our shoulders, turn our ankles, before we settle in again. Peter looks at his watch. First light is pearly blue at the horizon. He nods and lifts his rifle. 6:14 AM.

We settle in again for maybe ten minutes. It's hard to tell. I never wear a watch because I can't believe how time fools me out here. I will think I have been sitting absolutely dead still for maybe half an hour and only five minutes will have passed. Then I hear not one, maybe not even two, but several deer coming up the lower road, where I heard the first deer this morning. I signal, raise three fingers, shrug, maybe. Peter is all business now. Quickly, in one motion and without a sound, he raises the rifle to his shoulder and looks at the path through the scope. Now I hold my breath, transfixed on the dark alders before me. They seem to take shape before my eyes, bark turning dark green, foliage silver, as the light now pours down even before the sun has climbed above the trees. It happens so fast I never even see it. A young buck bursts out of the alders, leaping ahead of two smaller deer. He's coming right at us, then veers sharply left, turning downhill again. In that instant, Peter fires one shot. The buck continues forward down the hill. The other two deer leap away in opposite directions, one running past me so close I could nearly touch it. I can smell the warm rank fur. Peter is up and following the buck downhill. The sun breaks over the trees, spilling golden light. I run to catch up with Peter. Beside the lower path, the buck lies crumpled, its front legs folded under its chest, its head to one side. It's a clean kill, the perfect neck shot. The deer is dead. I touch its side, always surprised that it is not soft and velvety, as it looks, but coarse, rough short hairs. He's a spike, just two small points, probably a hundred twenty-five pounds. His coat is rich and glossy, healthy.

Peter kneels beside the deer like a suppliant. He doesn't say a word but strokes the muzzle softly, the ears. He stands. He rolls the buck over on to its back and splays its legs. He takes out his knife and with one careful, skillful incision, cuts around the testicles and up the middle all the way to the rib cage. Spreading the hide, he exposes the organs, completely intact. There is no blood. He has not nicked anything inside. In one motion, he gathers the internal organs, cutting away the heart and lungs, and sweeps them out onto the grass beside the buck. He takes a piece of rope out of his pocket, ties it to the buck's hind legs, and hangs him from a hornbeam tree, his nose about a foot above the ground. Peter has tremendous strength.
He swings the carcass up with such ease. The vital deer running up the hill just moments before is now gutted, a piece of meat hanging from a tree.

Peter turns to the organs, kneels before the stomach, slices it open.

"See," he says, the first word he's spoken since we left the house. "Look at that." The buck's stomach, the size of a soccer ball, is packed full with acorns, apples and sweet green clover, all proof that Peter's deer habitat plan is working. He is very proud of how healthy and well fed his deer are. He smiles.

We both stand then in what has become a sunny, bright morning. Another day. The dark mystery of our early morning vigil seems to have happened in another life. Peter will go down to the barn and get the four-wheeler to carry the buck out. I will stay here to guard the prize.

I sit back on a rock, not too close to the deer, but just so I can see it. I try to recreate the oneness I had felt earlier with the world around me, the keenness of my senses, the focus and capacity. Perhaps I need that lack of light, limiting my choices, as the imposed silence with Peter limits my expectations. Now I can see everything around me. Several feet away, a vole hurries through the grass, leaving a small trail through the drying frost. A blue jay calls from the top of a pine. Mourning doves coo somewhere below me. The pond glints through the trees further down, reflecting morning.

I heard the coyotes run almost every night those winters I spent in Limington. When I look back on it, I realize my listening then meant gathering strength. Preparing myself. It seems now I could only recognize how alien my presence was in Limington by giving myself over to the coyotes' nightly calls. By listening. Being in Limington with Peter was a foray into a wild world where ultimately I did not belong. On some level I wanted to believe that I was at one with nature, that I could exist in a world of the senses and connect with wild animals. There are times when I do connect with wild things, but I know now that I cannot live wholly within their sphere. I know now what I did not know then, that I require language and discourse. The silence of my relationship with Peter stunned me. It made me listen on a level I had never needed before to acknowledge the nuances between a man and a woman. It made me lonely. Loneliness needs less than two. And, in the silence that had settled like the snow over our house, blowing under the sills into every neat corner of our lives, I heard the coyotes run.

They lived in dens on the bank of the Little Ossipee River, about a mile below the tree farm, at the base of meadows across the Boothby Road. Every winter night around seven, when the stars burned in the sky and the snow began to creak and shrink as the temperature sank, the pack started up across the meadows, entering Peter's land below the pond by the logging road in the old orchard east of the house.

I would be in the kitchen then, moving back and forth in warm yellow light, finishing the dinner dishes. Alone. I remember turning off the running water and hearing that first yip-yip-yip above the moaning of the pines. Sometimes a coyote call sounds like a loon. There's a flutter, the first calls. The o-o-o-o-oh howl. Then silence. Was that a loon? Then the answering chorus, that blood-chilling vibrato. That was no loon. One coyote might not be so impressive, but a pack of them grabs your heart like a cold hard fist.

I came to love the nightly coyote runs. I paused in my life, suspended, waiting as if for a signal, a sound that could penetrate those decorous walls. I listened for the coyotes, visualized their progress, seeing in their dark passage under the frozen stars an obverse mirror of my own life masquerading in the hot, bright house. When I heard those cries, I was lifted up and out, my spirit soaring above the pines.

I imagined the pack heading first up through the apple trees. I heard them calling back and forth, saw them loping up the logging road, heads down, tails up, furtive even in numbers. They wind around the pond, big stone walls on one side, backlit by the snow as they pass through the clear-cut. I rinsed out the dishcloth and turned off the kitchen lights, soothed by their quest.

An hour later, reading by the wood stove, I heard them again, up on the ridge delineating the back border of the tree farm, The Oakes. Here, boulders no one man could move cluster on the ridge. Tall straight trees, hundreds of years old, reach to the sky. The coyotes were further away then, fainter. Perhaps they reconnoitered under those ancient trees, tongues lolling. I laid aside my book and looked at my blurred reflection in the frosted window. Beyond it, they must be sitting on the ridge, scrambling over the boulders, howling to the heavens, frosty clouds rising above their heads as starlight glints off the icy crust. I touched the cold pane with one reaching finger, melting a circle to look out into the night. Hopeful.

South of The Oakes, the land falls away into blueberry barrens and a mossy moraine. Here the pack spent the night, hunting rabbits, mice, even an occasional deer among the scrub pine. For several hours there was the intent silence of the hunt, the lull of the feast. I poked the fire, building it up for the night, thinking of their noses curled into bushy tails under a high chill moon.

Around three, the pack started down through the spruce stands of the old plantation on the western boundary. I woke then and turned, saw out the window next to our bed the iced pond fringed by black fir, hear their cries growing nearer, the yip-yip-yip more insistent as the pack was called in, tightened up for its final descent across the road and open meadows, down to their dens on the bank of the Little Ossipee. The distant call of predation. Sometimes, late in winter, I actually saw them, early in the morning, slipping down the frozen corn stubble, gray shadows melting into dark willows on the riverbank.

I should have been afraid. Once I met a coyote in broad daylight on a trail not far from the house. It lifted its head and looked me right in the eye. Kinship? Lots of people don't like coyotes. But they did me no harm. They left my chickens for the foxes, my cats for the fishers. And they called out to me. Made me feel sly. Cunning. Their wild blood pounding in my ears. I loved the loop they made around me all those winter nights, defining, it seems now, the limits of my life inside those walls, the confines of my possibilities there. Their cries made more sense to me than any human voice I heard.

    Regret stalks growth. It took me years to recognize I had made a choice, not a mistake, when I moved to Limington to live with Peter. What I didn't know about myself when I answered that personal ad, when I presented myself to him as "an interesting, intelligent *female*" who "enjoyed nature, literature, sunsets, sunrises, fine dining, travel" was that this was true. And my being with Peter in Limington, learning the seasons, following the deer, listening to the coyotes, put me in touch with that part of myself. It just wasn't enough. When I emerged from the woods and made my way back to the coast, I traveled a path forward. I had become a person who could, finally, imagine who she might be, not who she had been. No regrets. Only hope.

I approach the deer. A puddle of blood is congealing under its nose. I have never killed a deer, although I have seen them killed before. I cannot imagine lifting a gun to my shoulder, seeing this deer through the scope and pulling the trigger. Yet I am thrilled when Peter does. What am I doing here? I hear the four-wheeler coming up the logging road. A great blue heron sails between two pines at the far end of the pond below me. Incongruous and jarring. The rock I am sitting on rolled and tumbled under the ice sheet eons ago. This sun has burned holes in a million hearts. Just off the path beyond the hanging deer, I see a white glimmer in the sedge. Under a winter-blooming witch hazel, its fuzzy yellow buds just coming, lies the skeleton of a dead deer, nearly intact. I move the branches aside. Beautiful as architecture, ribs curve up from its spine, reaching above the bleached sweet grass. The delicate hoof is half eaten away by mice. Tiny, neat teeth in even rows decorate the jaw like scrollwork.

Mucking About

When I first met Elliot Gray in Maine and he told me he walked in the swamp in Florida, I never dreamed he was being literal.

"You don't really walk *in the swamp*," I had said, visualizing floating walkways above the murky waters of the Everglades.

"Absolutely, I do," he answered, and described old sneakers and long pants tucked into high socks, how he stepped around unseen cypress logs and skirted floating islands.

"There's two deputies I take out," he continued, "two female deputies. We were crossing this open area and one of them said to me, 'Elliot, stop!' I froze. Right between my legs was the biggest water moccasin I've ever seen. White mouth opened up at me. I picked up my foot and stepped back. Real slow."

"That was in the swamp?" I asked.

"Oh no. That was on the way to the swamp. You get in there, and you can't tell there are moccasins in the water or not. Probably not. But we walk through the water. It's about thigh high. It's like nothin' you ever did before. I take out all kinds of folks, even ones like you, good-looking well-preserved women who write about nature." He smiled at me. "You're gonna love it."

He's a handsome man in his early seventies, who looks at least ten years younger—my age—lean, bearded, his vanity betrayed by a collection of stylish, wide-brimmed hats, like the one he was wearing right then, soft suede with a rawhide strap. If I didn't go to Florida every winter to visit my ailing father in the Keys, I would never have even considered his offer. But there was something about Elliot, something about his passion for the experience that compelled me. Encouraged me. I could imagine myself walking through a swamp even as I never thought I would actually do it. I could talk about doing this, could tell people I was going to go "muck about," but somehow not really believe I was going to. A real life suspension of disbelief.

Seven or eight years earlier, Elliot and his wife Marion decided to drive down south one winter, and ended up in Southern Florida, not far from the Fakahatchee. They lived in their camper and volunteered as rangers in the Big Cypress National Preserve, picked up trash and watched the alligators. Elliot was bitten by the swamp bug. He took a nature walk one day in thigh-high water and never looked back. He and Marion were befriended by Clyde Butcher, a fine arts black and white nature photographer who runs the Big Cypress Gallery in Ochopee on twelve acres formerly the site of an orchid nursery. In return for winter housing, Butcher hired Elliot to capture all of the exotic plants that had been released there, and to bring the land back to as near indigenous as possible in a place where things sprout and bear fruit overnight in the fetid air. Butcher's oversized, compelling images captured with a nineteenth-century large-format view camera, brooding clouds over vast empty sharp-toothed wetlands, provided the perfect romantic vision of the swamp where Elliot was now totally immersed.

I had only recently met Elliot and Marion, old friends from my new husband's former life in western Maine, but his leading and her following were apparent immediately. They went to high school together in the tiny mountain town where the Appalachian Trail cuts over from New Hampshire into Maine. Old time Yankees. While Elliot pursued a career Marine life, she raised five children all over the globe before coming home to Maine to retire. He is one of those guys who got better looking and more interesting as he grew older. Marion, untouched by their worldly travels, drifted into rural dowdiness. She's a plain woman with a rough manner and a smoker's rasp. Four times she beat cancer. She's just come through a siege with number five, and the fear shows in her eyes.

The day I visited them in Maine, and Elliot invited me to come on a muck-about, he also told me he wanted to move to Florida year round and live in the swamp. In their New England living room, full of braided rugs and antimacassars, dark heavy furniture and drapes, Elliot brought out rattlesnake skins and the bones of southern predators. Marion knit mittens for the grandchildren and Elliot looked away. Outside, in the dooryard, he told me, "Marion doesn't really like the heat. She's not quite ready for Florida year round." Her cancer was not in remission and a series of treatments and surgeries was planned for early winter. Elliot pulled at his beard and said he would miss the orchid bloom, but he still hoped to be in the swamp to lead the New Year's Day Muck-About.

"I have to be there," he said, looking off at Sawyer's Mountain where the white birches, stripped of their leaves, gleamed like silver candelabra above the black conifers below. His eyes were clouded and gray as the northern sky. Inside, Marion's needles clicked in autumnal orange acrylic.

My motivation for this adventure is difficult to articulate. Even though I visit Florida every year to see my father, I continue to be jarred by its difference from home, from Maine, never quite able to move seamlessly from one to the other. I always have a disconnected feeling when I'm in Florida. I want to understand that. I had told myself that maybe more of an entry experience into the Keys would help; maybe it would be better if I drove down from the mainland rather than just stepping off a plane in Key West. Elliot's swamp is an easy halfway between Tampa and the Keys. There is something weird about Florida, something I can't quite get my head around I thought might be revealed if I entered it more slowly.

But driving down from Tampa this morning, I am still unsettled. My father had a stroke last year and he's deteriorating. This could be my last trip. I'm feeling guilty I've decided to stop off and "muck about" rather than get straight to him. But confronting him since the stroke is hard for me. His disability has removed any hope there may have been for us to resolve our deep differences. Driving now, I realize it's not Florida that jars and disconnects me; it's my unresolved relationship with my father. Unspoken words swirl around our encounters. Whatever his side of this conversation I run over and over in my head might be is locked within the tangled fibers of his brain's twisted and clotted dead-end arteries. Nuance is gone. The most I can hope for now is recognition. Never reparation. He has disappeared into confusion and taken my just anger with him. And though this trip I had resolved to "be there" for him, already I find myself taking a detour, avoiding our short-circuited reality in favor of the unknown swamp.

First light lit a Panther Crossing sign when I turned off Alligator Alley onto Route 41, about an hour north of Ochopee. I shivered. I could sense golden eyes unblinking in the tall grasses lining the road, just beyond the ten-foot fences the Florida Highway

Department has erected to save the panthers from becoming roadkill. They say there are fewer than a hundred panthers left. Pretty pricey protection for only a handful of big yellow cats. A few years earlier I'd met a man at a poetry reading who told me the new highway between Bangkok and Kuala Lampur was littered with dead tigers splattered by the big logging rigs roaring up out of the rain forest to fuel the Thai housing boom. He had painted a picture in my head: straight silver asphalt slashed through the vivid green jungle, big black and orange carcasses lining the sidings. Whenever I met someone who'd been to Southeast Asia, I asked about the tigers on the road to Kuala Lampur. Every one of them looked at me as if I were crazy. Didn't I know the tigers were protected? He wasn't even a poet, just a lawyer hanging out, hoping to score, but he'd gotten inside my head. Elliot's stories of his swamp had gotten inside my head too, and here I was about to stop imagining what it would be like to walk through a swamp, through thigh-high water full of snakes and alligators, and actually do it. I had come this far on a whim and somebody else's passion.

When I arrive, Elliot is standing alongside the driveway of Clyde Butcher's art gallery off Route 41, just outside the Big Cypress National Preserve. The way is thick with black mangrove and live oak, overhung by Spanish moss, the local ubiquitous epiphyte. Elliot is knee-deep in impatiens, running a weed whip. Wearing fatigues with a flack vest, high boots, and a becoming wide-brimmed straw hat, he looks the part for going native with style in the Everglades. When I tell him that, he smiles.

"I actually have quite a following down here. All sorts of people. Intellectuals. You'd be surprised." His body and aspect seem to have softened in the tropical air. He's different from the man I met in Maine last fall. Looser. He moves easily through the warm wet air, untouched by the humidity, seeming to feed off it like the epiphytes around him. An air man. Elliot has blossomed in the swamp, taking on the musk and exotica like one of the orchids he knows all about now, swinging at the end of a slender vine high up above his northern life.

Marion's surgery caused them to get down a little late this year. But Elliot made it one day before the New Year's Day Muck-About. At their cabin behind the gallery, he proudly shows me a picture of the group he led into the swamp. It's one of Butcher's eerie masterpieces, at least four feet by five feet, too big for the room. Eight men and women flank Elliot standing waist-deep in water under the gigantic fronds of a saw palmetto, fronted by a cypress log. Later I will think this is the only one of Clyde's photographs I have ever seen with human figures. Marion is not included.

She smiles and twists her fingers.

"We meet such interesting people down here," she says, "they're just so, so interesting."

"I check 'em out," Elliot tells me. "They'll call me from up at the gallery and say they have a group that wants to go out. I go up and talk to them. If I like the looks of them, we make a date. If I don't, then I make up an excuse." He smiles and runs his hands over his knees. Marion, her scalp shining through a post-chemo fuzz of gray, her eyes enormous, looks out the window of their cabin where the jungle encroaches and geckos scurry. He flexes his shoulders and tips his hat back with one finger. He looks like Indiana Jones. She looks like Indiana Jones' mother.

"There's a lot of important people." He smiles. "Photographers, nature writers. They like me." He looks down and then directly at me. "I don't know why."

I don't reply. Nor look away. And I don't know why either. It's not that I'm uncomfortable with Elliot or even that I think he's coming on to me. I'm not sure what's up here. He knows I'm a nature writer. What is he saying?

"Well," I answer finally, breaking our locked gaze and what has become an awkward silence. "They must know you'll show them the real thing." Marion relaxes and looks at Elliott. He stands and heads for the door.

"That's what it's all about," he replies, going out without looking back. I follow him. Marion hangs in the doorway. There's not much difference here, in or out. Just a filmy door separating the indoor screened view of the outdoor swaying trees and mosses. I linger with her, half way between in and out, wondering just what I've gotten myself into. I have a sense of her need to resist the aggressive growth around her, to wrap her arms around her frail body and stay safe in the house.

"Go on," she urges me. "It's wonderful out there." She touches my arm. Her fingers are like ice, startling in this close heat. "I've spent so much time in the swamp." She smiles sweetly. "Go on, there's nothing to be afraid of."

"I don't swim in lakes because they're 'funny' on the bottom," I tell her, letting the door close softly between us, a shushed whisper. "I must be out of my mind."

"Go," she says. "Lunch will be waiting." As she steps back from the screen, she fades from my view like the inverse of a photograph developing, her outlines blur, and only her eyes are visible, shining bright and clear as they catch light from between the trees. I nod and step off the porch, head down the soft needled path to where I can see Elliot waiting for me.

He gives me a walking stick. "That's the one rule we have," Elliot says. "You can't go in the swamp without a stick. It's your third leg." He's right about that. I wouldn't be able to make it without one. While the swamp isn't muddy or sticky, the going underwater is uneven. Unseen holes, logs, are hidden under silt, the bottom shifts and moves away beneath our feet. We need to lean on our sticks, to pull ourselves forward, test the depth of the next step. Elliot has mostly been quiet, looking around, looking back to see that I'm right behind him. I watch him carefully, stepping exactly as he steps, settling into his ripple ahead of me, keeping pace. The silence, like the silt, swirls around us, backwashing as it rolls up against the cypresses.

The day is overcast with just a hint of fog at the edges. Gnarled and twisted branches weave in and out of one another, mostly gray or silvery sage. It's February, so the new cypress hasn't leafed out yet. The only green comes from sword ferns surrounding the trees, fanning out four, five feet high like inverted tutus. They are reflected in the silky water, duplicating the fringed effect. Spiky bromeliads cluster halfway up tree trunks, congregate in hollows, hang off broken branches. Palmettos sheer up from unseen islands. The overall sense is symmetry and sharpness. No softness here, no rounded tufts. The cypresses are jagged. The palms are saw-toothed. The air flowers stab.

Swamp water is full of tannin from all the leaves decomposing in it, pleasantly cool and surprisingly clear, except as we stir it up. My legs in khaki pants appear bronzed, shimmer beneath the surface. We are surrounded by the shredding trunks of cypress trees. We bow under low branches. Yellow bladderwort swirls ahead of us. Bright green duck weed floats on either side.

I can see that even in the water we are on a path, that someone has gone here before us. Elliot says if you make a path, everyone will use it, that it's the nature of things, especially animals, to take the easiest route. I wonder when I hear him say that whether he's talking about himself. Watching Elliott stride easily ahead of me now down this watery path, what I feel is his drawing away from Marion, his need to distance himself from the death of her flesh and their long life together. I can feel him turning, a rare orchid, a tender shoot, toward the sun of the living. For him too, it seems, this ever-changing path is, as he has said, the easiest route, firmer ground, perhaps, than what he finds on land. As we follow the narrow swath of open water between thick floating plants, I picture what has come here before us: deer, surely; all the long-legged walking birds; maybe even a panther. In my mind, I can see them all wending their way through the swaying mosses and reaching vines, fading one by one into the gloom. I see myself in this progression, following in their wake, stepping into their rippling steps even as I do now into Elliot's. Just so.

I can't get over how calm I am. It's as if by talking about it, by telling everyone I was going to Florida to walk in a swamp, I have allowed myself to do this. The swamp soothes me. The silken water, the sentient air, moist and caressing, the muted light, lustrous as a pearl. I let out my breath and pick up my head, dare to look around. The beauty of the swamp is exotic and primitive, especially to a northerner. And I'm a northerner, through and through. For me, it's dreamlike to be standing in the water under these eldritch trees full of plants, open and relaxed, nodding like a pollinator. I can feel my lungs adjust to the wet air, expanding, eagerly sucking up the green oxygen, pushing it out and through my body. Each breath sluices away the clenched cold, bellows through me to slough off winter's dead skin until I emerge, pink as an orchid, reborn: a person who walks through swamps in Florida. The parsimony of the country of the pointed firs doesn't allow for such greed in nature. Our northern swamps are really bogs, or peat lands, developed where water drainage was blocked and decomposition slowed and took over. They are high in acidity, low in oxygen: northern swamps are repositories of dead life. Landlocked, they fulminate testimony to the past: pollen grains trapped in an air bubble from antiquity. This southern swamp seethes with life. It smells like semen.

Suddenly we hear the call of a barred owl, very close. Elliot stops. An answering call comes from the opposite direction.

"We saw this fella last week," he says as he scans the trees around. The swamp offers no clear vistas. Vegetation at eye level is sparse this time of year, but numerous trees and shrubs loom over us, a crazy crosshatch of branches and trunks. It's hard to see very far away. Doubly hard because everything looks the same. Whichever way I turn are cypress trees, hanging Spanish moss, and broken branches. I understand Elliot's GPS. Any guideposts here are not evident to the uninitiated.

We hear another answering call from behind us. We stop again and look around. Then, not a dozen feet away and about ten feet up, a barred owl, soft and beige as a moth, flies right past us. Its wing spread is at least four feet. How such a big bird can fly between these trees, could have been so close to us and yet unseen, amazes me. So much here is evident yet not discernible. Obvious, yet hidden. We stop and turn and follow the owl's progress until it is lost, blending into the trees.

Elliot tells a story about Oscar, another guide in the preserve, whose Indian name is Speaks with Owls, about his calling in the barred owls.

"That's probably Oscar teasing us," he says. I don't like thinking one of the calls I heard was some guy making like an owl. I want there to be two owls, two of those glorious striped creatures winging about this maze. We begin to move forward. Then, right above us there is a rustle. We look up to see a barred owl sitting on the branch of a cypress tree, blinking, turning its funny short tufted neck, peering down at us with huge golden eyes. This time I take a picture. Speaks with Owls indeed. Something in me likes Elliot's having been proved wrong.

He shrugs. "I get along with Oscar now," he says. "Last year, I didn't like him. We had a competition. He does his thing, I do mine. I do whatever I want." I don't respond. He doesn't seem to require an answer. It's as though he's talking to himself, continuing a familiar dialogue that has nothing to do with me but rather his need to convince himself. After a lifetime of being paired, Elliot is readjusting, talking himself into a single stance, part of his distancing from Marion. He will survive. He will do whatever he wants. I understand Elliot's need to distance himself from the decay of his household and to immerse himself instead in the transmogrifying swamp. My husband told me before I met Elliot that his job in Vietnam was to bring home the body bags. "Can you imagine?" my husband had exclaimed. I watch Elliot moving through this moody jungle with ease, familiarity. Yes. I can imagine. Elliot has carried the dead before.

The swamp is settling into my shoes. Not mud, just wet. The soothing feeling I had earlier is fading. I feel isolated now, not knowing where I am. I don't feel lost. I feel irrevocably separated from all of my ordinals. More, I realize how useless they are to me. In a way, it's freeing. Like Elliot's trying on his single life. I see how the swamp assists him in that, equalizes loss and hope. Standing in the sweet water, surrounded by warm gray air, the shifting landscape, I realize I am not afraid. Forty years ago, when I was a poetic college student, I used to say I loved the fog because it showed things the way they really were, shrouded, unclear. A typical literary conceit. But standing in the swamp I am reminded of that young dictum of mine, of how I have finally come 'round to a place where it might actually be true! I like that. It helps me to feel calm again. Whatever there may be to fear in this world is not in this place. Marion was right. I step forward with confidence, hurrying to catch up with Elliot. My foot slips off an unseen log, and I nearly fall over. Well, that's not fear. That's just carelessness. Gripping my stick firmly, I pull myself upright again, remember to test the water ahead of me, and move forward with sureness.

The land takes on a different aspect. It is as though we have climbed up on to a plateau in the swamp. We are still walking through water, but it is shallower here, just up to our knees, and the path we take is much more obvious, winding like a river through fields of short gray sedge. I realize this is a hammock, one of those ridges of elevated ground that occur here near the Everglades, an island of explosive vegetation, hurried growth mere inches above sea level.

We hear a sharp, guttural sound. I turn to Elliot. He points ahead to where a cloud of white flutters through the distant cypress branches. A flock of white ibis, more than a hundredfold, wheels, settles, chatters its barking call, rises, flutters in, stands atop the tallest trees. The ibis is a big bird, probably two feet tall with a wider wing span. In flight it resembles the heron, long neck extended, long legs stretched out behind. In the air, the birds keep to a pattern, turn as one, settle in a group, fall from the sky like huge snowflakes drifting among the branches to find a space. Alighted, they all face in the same direction. I crane my neck to see what they might be looking at. They rise and fall, fly up and down on some secret current of the wind, following an arcane mission known only to them. As we approach, they take flight all at once, a thunder, and we turn to see them light again, performing the same dance over and over.

Some years before I had been invited to visit a rare great blue heron rookery in an ancient preserved forest in northern Maine. The great birds swooned in and out among hundred-foot-high pine trees over three centuries old. I was there because a forester wanted me to write about how carefully his company was husbanding this secret growth. He pointed out everything special and nurturing in the selective cutting, but what I saw were the stark twisted skeletons of baby herons that had fallen from their nests on high, heaped at the feet of trees too big to put my arms around. Their bleached white eyes peered blind from bony, grasping beaks. All around them were aqua shards as big as my hands from the burst eggs of their brethren, hopeful in the nests above. At home, I still have a picture on my desk of those skeletons right next to a luminous, glowing shell fragment. I never did write that story. The white ibis mirror the herons like a photograph negative, and just as obverse, seem more assimilated than the dark herons, more in possession of their place, less awkward in their aspect. The soft south. The cold north. The live swamp. The dead bog.

We turn and cross the hammock, heading downhill into darker territory. Now the growth is thicker again. We have left behind the poisonwood, scrub mahogany. Overhead a red-shouldered hawk flies, crying loudly.

"That's my buddy," Elliot says. "He likes to see me come. He knows I stir things up." The hawk circles and lands on a tree ahead of us, still crying its high-pitched grating call. Just beyond this tree, the undergrowth opens up to reveal a fairly good-sized pond, maybe half an acre, surrounded by sabal palm and fringed all around by Virginia chain fern. In the center it is black, not the tea-brown water we have seen before. No plants are growing there.

"Know what that means?" Elliot asks me.

"Yes," I say quickly. "The water is deep."

He grimaces.

"That's right," he concedes. He hasn't gotten me back for the barred owl yet. His buddy the red-shouldered hawk mocks him overhead. Elliot grins and shrugs.

"Well, now we have some choices," he says, leaning on his stick. "We can skirt this pond, take maybe an hour, hour and a half, or we can head around the other way and get back to base in about forty-five minutes."

Elliot has offered to show me where a big rattler, maybe six feet, lives in the hollow of a tree, but that's way on the other side of this pond and somehow, now that I'm out here, I'm not so eager to approach the snake's home turf. While the going isn't hard, it is tense, tiring, and I'm beginning to feel uncomfortable with wet feet.

"Your call," Elliot says.

I know that Marion is making lunch. She has already called in on the walkie-talkie and I heard him tell her a while back we'd be in soon. Skirting the pond would not be soon.

"I think I'm ready to head in. Let's not keep Marion waiting too long," I say. Elliot is still leaning on his stick. He doesn't respond.

"How's she really doing, Elliot?" I ask him.

"Oh, she's OK. Some days good, some days bad. She's a fighter. She'll be all right." He talks fast, not looking at me, scanning the treetops instead, actually swiveling his head around.

"Elliot?" He turns then and looks me in the eye. "I'm sorry," I tell him. "I can't imagine this slow draining of you both. I've been so 'lucky' in my deaths, they've all been sudden—"

"OK, let's do it." He cuts me off and turns. He passes me, a foot away and hesitates. I want to enfold him, put my arms around him and let him relax into my soft female body. We stand there, gentle ripples of swamp water washing up our thighs.

He moves ahead abruptly. "Watch your step," he says. Silently, I fall in behind him. I'm shocked at my reaction. In the water, Elliot is too close.

Even though I've said more than two hours in the swamp is enough for me this first time out, and even though Marion must have lunch waiting, Elliot wants to show me a clump of rare cigar orchids. He stops and starts, checks his compass, punches in some numbers on the GPS.

"Snake," he laughs. "I got the big rattlesnake on here. Guess I didn't put the orchids in." It seems to me we're circling, but even though I can usually find my way fairly well in northern woods, I am literally at sea here. And there's no sun.

I begin to lag behind, looking carefully at every tree for as far as I can see. I know what the orchids look like, a starburst of cylinders, like big Cuban cigars sprouting maybe a foot up from the stump of a tree. I would love to see them before Elliot does. When we first left the cabin on our way to the swamp, he had pointed out the different species of orchid high above, seemingly suspended in midair from the bark of big old mangroves. Mostly what he showed me were bright green vines twined around the branches of the trees, leafless. Only a few were just coming back into bloom after the midwinter hiatus. Now, in the swamp, Elliot points out more vines, some even with leaves, describes the miraculous flowers that will soon appear above us but are nowhere evident at this moment. The grass pink is early, rewarding him, its magenta butterfly-shaped petals clustered on high—long, loose and leafless. These airy flowers look so much less zenlike here where they belong than where I'm used to seeing them, bonsaied in pricey pots with one artistic rock at northern florists. I've never seen orchids growing wild before.

Elliot points out sawn stumps of cypress trees, sawn logs lying in the water. "Poachers," he spits. In Maine, we have deer poaching, but it's hard for me to imagine people slogging through a swamp in order to steal flowers. "Cut the whole tree down for the cigar orchids up high. Damn!" Elliot stops and stares at the mutilated cypress. "You know," he says without turning around, "these orchids are just as protected as the panthers. Maybe more. People used to chop 'em down, like this, and send them up north to be centerpieces for fancy dinners, big log right in the middle of the table. Probably still do for all I know. Damn!" He stomps on, the water roiling away from him.

By now we've passed back through the hammock of swamp prairie and begun to follow one of the streams in a direction even I can tell is different from the way we came in.

"This water is always moving," Elliot says. "Spit in this water and your spit will travel southeast." I look down at the golden stillness circling my legs. I don't feel any current.

"It's not tidal, is it?" I ask.

"Naw." Elliot turns away and pushes on. I hang back and quietly spit into the water behind me. I stand and watch. Slowly, slowly, my saliva circles, begins to move toward the side, edges into the grass and disappears behind a stick. Southeast. This water wants to live in Florida City.

Up ahead, we can see a tangle of mangrove, huge spiky swordtail fern. Elliot stops and says, "We're going to pass about four or five feet from Mister Big, so let's keep quiet." Just before we entered the swamp, we had skirted a pond where Elliot pointed out the native flora along its edges, alligator flag and lizard's-tail, those bottlebrush-like fragrant flowers drooped over at the top, looking like fluffy white lizards poking their heads up above the big heart-shaped leaves.

"There's a ten-footer lives in here," he had said, gesturing toward the pond. "We call him Mister Big." I had looked all across the glassy surface for something resembling an alligator.

"He's shy," Elliot had said when he noticed me looking. "He's down under those pond apple branches. You won't see him until he wants to see you." As he turned away down another path, I couldn't help looking back to see if Mister Big was peering at us from the dark edge of the pond, poking his nose up above the lizard's-tails. Not a ripple.

"So what do I do, Elliot, if Mister Big comes toward me?" I ask now. Elliot turns and flashes a smile.

"Just push him away with your stick. Nudge him in the opposite direction." Nudge? Nudge a ten-foot alligator? I actually do misstep and make a splash, but I don't try to cover it. Elliot turns, annoyed.

"Sorry," I say, but I am relieved to see that from under the branches of the pond apple there is no ripple, no interest from Mister Big.

Within a minute we have gained the shore and are up on dry land again, just a few feet from the path where we entered. We see the cabin through the leaves. Marion is waiting next to it. Even though she wears shorts, a flax pullover, she's pale and doesn't look as though she belongs here. Certainly not next to Elliot, tanned in his fatigues, his rakish hat.

"Oscar just took a group out," she tells him.

"Who? Who'd he take?" Elliot wants to know.

She shrugs. "Someone."

We change our wet clothes, sit around in what they call the Florida room down here, a big open space with floor-to-ceiling windows. We eat the ham salad sandwiches and New England clam chowder Marion has prepared for us. No fresh vegetables, no fruit. It's a northern winter lunch, willful, as though she refuses to acknowledge that only a few miles away are farm stands with luscious red tomatoes, delicious sweet strawberries, still warm from the sun.

Elliot passes around beautifully produced books of color photographs of the local flora and fauna, pointing out the photographers he's taken into the swamp. The books are heavy and glossy, pornographic in their exquisite exotic intimacy. Close-ups of the golden eyes of panthers. Dewy, pollen-laden blooms of orchids. Detail of the crosshatch on an alligator's foot.

"Read the inscription," Elliot says to me, opening one to the frontispiece. "See what she said about me." The text is voluminous, written in a flowery, aggressive hand that covers nearly all the page. I cannot make out a single word, except "love," at the end.

Well past noon now, the sun has burned off the fog, leaving behind a bright humid closeness. It seems I have been here through a season. The day is getting on and I've promised my father I will be in the Keys before dark. I rise to say good-bye. Elliot seems diffident to me, looks away, as I turn toward the door.

"You can't stay?" Marion asks. She stands between us in the kitchen, framed by a glassed-in breakfast nook where gigantic fronds brush the windows. Backdrop for a panther sighting.

"I just want everything to get back to normal," she says awkwardly with the inappropriate candor of the dying. No time for niceties. She seems to recognize this and smiles apologetically. "Everything is so, so different here. Not like home."

"This is home," Elliot says, from the other room, where he stands before the window now. "I'm more at home here than anyplace I've ever been."

She turns back to me. "I just want some, what's the word? Normalcy. I want some normalcy."

Close by we hear the barred owl call.

"Damn that Oscar," Elliot mutters.

Back out on Route 41, heading out of Ochopee toward Florida City, I pass a wildlife park hidden behind scrub oak hanging over the road. Right next to the park, looming out of fronds of sabal and saw-toothed palm, is a huge plaster panther model. It's at least twenty-five feet long, maybe ten feet high. The cat is fully extended, its head bent forward attentively, tail extended. I pull into the parking lot and look over the rusted cages full of exotic birds, raccoons, even a red fox, pacing and gnawing at the wire. I don't go inside for the "believe it or not" products.

Up close, the plaster cat is cracked and peeling. But from the road, it looks pretty realistic. If you aim your camera carefully, you can frame the cat apart from anything to suggest its real proportions. I take just such a picture, startling in its immediacy: later, people will look at this photograph and think it is a real panther stalking in high grass.

So many things are not what they seem. And yet, some are exactly that: adventures in life and journeys of the imagination into territory so unknown we invent new ways of walking and seeing in order to assimilate the experience. I had been afraid to walk in the swamp, but there was nothing to fear there. I found instead a sense of peace in the soft water. The feeling I had of being out of time and place dissipates with every mile I put between myself and Elliot and Marion. Back on dry land. Firm footing. Yet I am speeding toward another dying situation. Orchids bloom and fade, only to return again. It takes seven years to germinate an orchid seed, seven years before you know if the plant will grow. Seven years of hope. Seven years of trust. In seven years, both Marion and my father will be gone. Will Elliot still need the swamp? Whose rippling footsteps will I be stepping into then?

Emerging from the sheltered preserve to drive toward my wordless father, I pass through miles and miles of Homestead's open garden land, all green and orderly. Despite the squeak of the swamp in my sandals, I am trying to move beyond landscapes that shift underfoot. Despite the fogged words and disconnection ahead, I will try to be there for my father. Along the road, farm after farm of exotic plants wait to be shipped north, so far beyond their habitat they will last less than a year there, just long enough to inflame the memory with a scent of soft air and high white sky.

Biography

Penelope Schwartz Robinson has been the director of an academic journals publishing company, a blue-water sailor, litigation paralegal, tree farmer, wife, mother, and grandmother. A graduate of the University of Michigan and the University of Southern Maine's Stonecoast MFA program, she has taught nonfiction literature and writing at the University of Maine, Farmington and Southern Maine Community College. Her honors include an Intro Award in nonfiction from the Association of Writers and Writing Programs, and a notable citation in *Best American Essays, 2005*. She lives in Cape Elizabeth, Maine, with her husband.

Publications Acknowledgment

The following essays appeared previously in these journals:

"Lofting," *Ascent*, Volume 29, Number 1, Fall, 2004.
   Moorhead, MN: Concordia College. (*Best Amercian Essays* Notable Essay, 2005)

"All Hands," *Willow Springs*, Volume 54, Summer/Fall, 2004.
   Cheney, WA: Eastern Washington University. (AWP Intro Award from the Intro Journal Project, 2004)

"Mucking About," *River Teeth, A Journal of Nonfiction Narrative*, Volume 8, Number 1, Fall, 2006. Lincoln, NE: University of Nebraska Press.

Praise for *Slippery Men*

"Penelope Schwartz Robinson's 'slippery' men—lovers, preachers, gardeners, swamp-muckers and fathers—are simultaneously endearing and suspect. In bringing them to life in these lyrical and trenchant pages, she is wise enough to look at her own foibles and complexities, and talented enough to transform her experiences into stories that amuse and instruct. This work is simply superb."
— Barbara Hurd, author of *Stirring the Mud: On Swamps, Bogs, and Human Imagination*

"Sometimes a voice gets in your head and in your heart, a voice that's true and observant and wonders hard about the way we live. Penelope Schwartz Robinson owns such a voice, and *Slippery Men* is an extraordinary book—filled with joy and grace and that insistent voice that makes each page an illumination."
—W. Scott Olsen, author of *Hard Air: Adventures from the Edge of Flying*

"In *Slippery Men*, Penelope Schwartz Robinson manages to be both clever and warm, a neat trick, and a real storyteller, too. Both women and men will smile at themselves in the mirror she holds up to contemporary life."
—Katha Pollitt, author of *Learning to Drive and Other Life Stories*

"Penelope Schwartz Robinson is a wise and wonderful tour guide into the landscapes of her life—from the mitt of Upper Michigan, to upstate New York, through Maine's woods, to a day mucking around a Florida swamp. Her prize-winning collection, at once lyrical and reflective, makes us see the power of place to reveal and to nourish who we are: along paths of beauty and darkness, silence and sound, loss and rejuvenation. A journey not to be missed!"
—Mimi Schwartz, author of *Good Neighbors, Bad Times, Echoes of My Father's German Village*

"The 'slippery' men Robinson writes about in these provocative—and evocative—essays remind us of the slipperiness of life itself. One moment we see Robinson face to face with a man she meets through a personal ad, the next we are back in childhood, floating in a boat with her (yes, slippery) father, 'drawn by the current's tug into a tunnel of dark water.' Time, men, and water all slip and slide through Robinson's life, but not through her fingers. She captures them all with a poignant, fleeting intensity in this stellar literary—and lyrical—debut."
—Sue William Silverman, author of *Because I Remember Terror, Father, I Remember You*

"*Slippery Men* is a bold investigation into the major events, places, and relationships that have helped shape the author's understanding of her place in the world. In this excellent collection, Penelope Schwartz Robinson shows herself to be a companionable guide and shrewd observer of human nature. The author's complex, courageous journey to selfhood is a story readers will both admire and identify with."
—Michael Steinberg, author of *Still Pitching*

main keep

814.54 ROBINSON
Robinson, Penelope
Schwartz.
Slippery men

WITHDRAWN

PORTLAND PUBLIC LIBRARY
5 MONUMENT SQ.
PORTLAND, ME 04101

DATE DUE		
MAR 31 2009		
APR 1 8 2009		